Archivists, Collectors, Dealers, and Replevin

Case Studies on Private Ownership of Public Documents

Elizabeth H. Dow

THE SCARECROW PRESS, INC.
Lanham • Toronto • Plymouth, UK
2012

Published by Scarecrow Press, Inc.
A wholly owned subsidiary of
The Rowman & Littlefield Publishing Group, Inc.
4501 Forbes Boulevard, Suite 200, Lanham, Maryland 20706
www.rowman.com

10 Thornbury Road, Plymouth PL6 7PP, United Kingdom

British Library Cataloguing in Publication Information Available

Library of Congress Cataloging-in-Publication Data

Dow, Elizabeth H.
Archivists, collectors, dealers, and replevin : case studies on private ownership of public documents / Elizabeth H. Dow.
pages cm
Includes bibliographical references and index.
ISBN 978-0-8108-8377-2 (cloth) — ISBN (invalid) 978-0-8108-8378-9 (ebook)
1. Public records—Law and legislation—United States. 2. Archives—Law and legislation—United States. I. Title.
KF5752.D69 2012
342.73'0662—dc23
2012008889

™ The paper used in this publication meets the minimum requirements of American National Standard for Information Sciences—Permanence of Paper for Printed Library Materials, ANSI/NISO Z39.48-1992.
Printed in the United States of America.

To Beth Paskoff

Contents

Preface

At the 2009 meeting of the Society of American Archivists (SAA), the Council of State Archivists (CoSA), a professional organization made up of the archivists of each state, sponsored back-to-back sessions on replevin (pronounced re PLEV in), a legal action brought for the purpose of recovering specified items.[1] The first session featured a panel of three state archivists, who discussed the problem of public documents that appear on the market and the problems each had encountered in retrieving them. The second consisted of a brainstorming session during which the participants shared ideas on ways to address the problem.

During the brainstorming session, the participants identified two problems that caused the most distress. In the first place, they have trouble convincing their state's Attorneys General (AG) to take legal action against people who hold public documents. For the AGs working with limited budgets, retrieving *alienated documents,* the term for public documents not stored in an archives, does not seem as compelling as negotiating to minimize water disputes in drought-prone areas or cooperating with federal agents in detecting and stopping terrorists. Archivists, who also work with inadequate budgets, understand the AGs' rationale, but it frustrates them.

In addition to the lack of enforcement support from AGs, archivists find that dealers in autographs and manuscripts often do not willingly cooperate with them. Dealers do not voluntarily disclose where they acquire the documents they sell or who buys them. Their business depends on trust between them and their buyers and sellers, and for dealers to reveal their sources and customer information puts them at risk of breaking essential links in the chain of contacts they need to do business. Many insist on a court order that compels them to respond to the archivists' inquiries.

1. Society of American Archivists. Annual Meeting. Washington, DC, Session 105 and 205, August 13, 2009.

Without the AGs' support in getting and enforcing court orders, archivists can do very little. However, as professionals charged with completing the historical records they have responsibility for, they want to get on with that task.

In 1948, a group of manuscript collectors and dealers created the Manuscript Society (MS), now the country's oldest and best known organization for manuscript collectors and dealers. The society publishes a newsletter, *Manuscript Society News*, and a quarterly journal, *Manuscripts*, through which members follow market trends and share stories about manuscripts. As part of its philanthropy, the Manuscript Society's Scholarship Committee offers support to scholars using manuscripts as the basis for their research, and its Replevin Committee offers support for members defending themselves against a replevin action. To the archivists at the SAA session, the Manuscript Society represented "the enemy" in their efforts to retrieve alienated documents.

Not surprisingly, the Manuscript Society sees CoSA as the enemy. When collectors and dealers see archivists demanding the return of documents individuals bought on the open market, claiming that the documents belong to the government and in a government archives, collectors and dealers see archivists exercising an unconscionable seizure of private property. They point to the centuries during which government at all levels cared for public documents poorly, if at all. They argue that by saving important historical documents, collectors have actually done the job that government officials abdicated. They see the recent enthusiasm among archivists for "completing the historical record" as too late and largely targeted at small dealers and collectors, subjecting them to the worst form of governmental bullying.

At the SAA meeting, part of the discussion focused on how much ignorance the players on both sides of the issues have about the role and use of replevin in the world of manuscript collecting and management. The archival educators at the meeting bemoaned the fact that between the limited time and the seemingly unlimited topics they must address in their classes, replevin, a fairly abstract concept to most students, does not get much attention. Archivists acknowledged that when approaching dealers and the lawyers in their own AG's office, their first challenge lies in explaining the problem. All agreed that a book of case studies would make explaining and discussing replevin of public documents much easier. I wrote this book to fill that need.

In the SAA discussion, I stood up to make a point about the Manuscript Society. As a shortcut to explain the basis of my knowledge, I said that I had married into the Manuscript Society and then said what I had to say. As I was leaving the room at the end of the session, I passed a table that CoSA had set up. The woman staffing the table looked at me, smiled, and said, "Sort of like marrying the Mafia, right?" I already knew how deep and raw the animosity toward archivists runs among manuscripts collectors and dealers. At that moment it struck me how deep and raw the animosity toward the Manuscript Society runs in CoSA. I immediately felt that something had to happen to reduce the tensions between the two groups.

Acknowledgments

My heartfelt thanks go to Ed Bomsey, David Chesnutt, Polly Darnell, David Haury, Bob Hopper, Ivo Meisner, Scott Petersen, Ken Rendell, David Rowell, James Travers, George Vogt, Julia Marks Young, and the many other dealers, collectors, and professional archivists who spoke to me with great candor.

Introduction

The past tugs at people in many ways and from many directions. David Lowenthal has written extensively on the question of what causes those tugs and how we respond to them.[1] He makes clear that we cannot ever truly know the past, so we cling to items from the past looking for all the information and evidence they can provide us about it. We do this as societies and as individuals. Government repositories document the activities of the governmental body they represent. Collecting repositories look for materials that fit their mission statements and collecting policies. Private collectors often have a passion for a particular person, topic, period, or type of document. Dealers seek to serve all three groups.

According to an article in the *Wall Street Journal* quoting Selby Kiffer, Sotheby's senior international specialist for books and manuscripts, "The overall auction market for rare American historical documents totals $30 million to $50 million annually, with roughly 5,000 to 8,000 pieces sold per year."[2] Note that the Kiffer figure reflects only auction sales; it does not include the value of those documents sold in private transactions. Heritage Auctions advertises auction sales including manuscripts of $600 million a year. For millennia, people have collected historical documents, impelled by a wide variety of motives.

Governments created much of the material that generates so much money, and by today's standards, that material belongs in government archives. Unfortunately, in the United States, governments at all levels came to the practice of collecting and protecting historical material only within the past century or so. Archives, by origin and nature, are government organs, and Americans tend to shy away from even minimum permanent government bureaucracy. Legislatures are slow to create and develop new government agencies or to grow those already in existence—especially when bureaucratic posts went to political appointees. In Iowa, one of the states whose legislators had a relatively early and lively interest in archives, "a prominent legislator expressed himself very characteristically during debates on appropriations for State archives: 'The greater portion of the documents are "junk" and should be dumped into the river. The object of the appropriation is to provide jobs for broken-down politicians.'"[3] Even when established, government archives performed poorly. Appointing workers to the archives using the spoils system meant an untrained and constantly changing workforce. That, in turn, precluded the development of a tradition of sound archival management and preservation. As a result, older records "were carelessly neglected by often wholly unsuitable officials, and no properly conducted department archives were set up."[4] Even when governments legislated good intentions, they rarely included adequate budgets and support to develop an archives and protect historical materials.

This history of legislative hesitation to develop government archives has produced a situation that today puts governmental archivists and manuscript collectors (both private collectors and collecting repositories) in conflict and competition for the government documents that come out of private hands and onto the market. Government archivists work under a variety of laws as to what they can define as theirs. Some laws specifically include documents back into colonial times; others don't mention time at all. Collectors and dealers assert that since governments didn't take care of their historical documents properly at the time of their creation, they should not have the right to claim them now because they might have left government control decades or centuries ago. Collectors point out that if not for the collectors who protected them, the documents would not exist at all. Collectors resent governments' applying a twenty-first-century perspective to the results of pre-twentieth-century caretakers' attitudes and behavior—both of which perfectly reflected the perspective of that era. This divide becomes especially acute around displayable "trophy" documents written by or about a person or event that tugs at everyone familiar with history.

The problem of *alienated* government documents (also called *estrayed* or *displaced* and *fugitive* documents) begins to appear in American archival literature as soon as American archival literature appears.[5] It has re-emerged in various guises since then. As one might expect, the archival literature on the topic always reflects the archivists' perspective. From the beginning authors took the position that archival materials should reside in the archives or some other form of public repository, such as a historical society or a university's Special Collections Department. After they had their facilities in place, government archivists would have preferred that manuscript curators in universities and historical societies empty their holdings of all public documents and turn them over them to a government archives. All writers agreed that public documents should not reside in the hands of private collectors.

Private collectors organized in 1948 as a gathering of hobbyists, not as a profession. Their literature reported replevin activity to keep collectors aware of the problem, but it offered no particular analysis of it.[6] Only twice have I found any theoretical discussion of the problem in the literature of the collecting community.[7]

I know of no work but this book that presents both sides of this issue and examines them dispassionately. Both sides have much to gain by understanding the other's perspective. Without that understanding, the two sides will be forever at war. States will pass laws, as many now have, forbidding the private ownership of public papers. Collectors and dealers will take important material underground, sell it to foreign buyers, or just destroy it.

This book will not serve as a legal guide. Since all the state and the federal government laws vary in their technicalities, such a book may never exist. This book will, however, provide a full discussion of the problem. In the first six chapters, it contains the complex context in which the problem lies. The first chapter reviews the history of institutional and state-sponsored collecting and care of historical documents in the United States. The second collects tales of theft and neglect that occurred in the process. The third covers the development of the archival profession in the United States. These first three chapters, taken together, explain the core points of contention that have grown out of the history. The fourth chapter reviews the phenomenon of collecting, both as a hobby and as an institutional activity. It reveals the deep emotional currents that come into play when a collection appears threatened. The fifth chapter provides a general review of both state and federal statutes on public documents in private hands. With that background in place, the sixth chapter distills the perspectives of the various parties in the struggle. The eighth chapter presents steps holders of public documents can take to avoid conflicts and steps an archives can take to protect its collection.

The seventh chapter presents a series of case studies developed to evoke the complexity of these conflicts. I cannot furnish a right or wrong answer to any of the cases; laws vary too much. Instead, I hope the cases provide an introduction to the issues and promote an understanding of the quandary both sides find themselves in. If I am successful, the reader will come away from the cases with an understanding of both positions and with ideas about what seems equitable to both sides. The actual cases come from my own imagination, although I based some on circumstances I've learned of in the course of my research. I have designed the cases to illuminate the problems and provoke an analysis of the thorny issues surrounding the conflicting claims on historical documents.

A Few Words

A word about *manuscript*. In this book, I use the term *manuscript* to represent a primary historical document, regardless its method of creation.

A word about manuscript and autograph *dealers*. Dealers specialize in selling documents by "a person of consequence." That makes them first and foremost business people. Much of their attitude about the conflict comes from their desire to run a smooth and profitable business. Some may also collect materials privately. All know a great deal about the autograph and manuscript market and public documents. Most know much less about the world of archives.

A word about *autograph*. Autograph refers to either a person's signature or a piece of writing in the hand of an individual. A handwritten document might also be called a manuscript, as institutional collectors use the term. The contents may or may not have historical value.[8]

A word about *organizational names*. This book focuses on a problem that several professional organizations have addressed. Many of those organizations have had more than one name over time. Rather than burden the reader with remembering the succession of names, I have chosen to use the current name throughout.

A word about the word *archives*. Like many English terms, archives has several meanings, and in conversational use, we generally rely on context to deduce the meaning conveyed in the moment. If we can't figure it out, we ask for clarification. In a published work, the reader can't ask for clarification, so the author must pick a meaning and stick with it. In this work, the term archives will refer to those materials of enduring value collected by governments to document their own history. I will refer to personal and family papers as *manuscript collections* and to organizations that collect historical documents as *collecting repositories.*

A word about *archivists.* Archivists work in archives, bearing the responsibility for the archives of their employers—in this case, a governmental body. *Manuscripts curators* work in collecting repositories.

A word about *collections*. Like archives, in archival circles, *collections* may have several meanings. In this work, collections means "a group of papers attributable to a single source." I use the term *holdings* for the "materials held by a repository."

A word about *records*. While definitions of the concept of a record vary, all include the fundamental concept that a record provides evidence of a transaction between two or more entities and may have legal implications. Governmental archives collect records to document their institution's activities and to defend themselves in case of a legal challenge.

A word about *state*. As a generic term, *state* can refer to any national or regional government. However, when I use it in this book, I'm referring to one or more states of the United States. For the larger union, I refer to the federal government, the United States, or the country.

A word about *ownership*. Because ownership of so many of the documents under discussion here is a matter of contention, I use the term *holder* to designate the party who has physical control of the materials.

About the Case Studies

The case studies in chapter 7 provide the motive for writing all that comes before and after them. I intend for them to serve as points of discussion. The first group provides an exercise in clarifying the distinction between a public and non-public documents. After that, both sides in the dispute have a case to make.

Discussants using a case study will have the opportunity to make the case for each and figure out what to do. I provide guiding questions generally and more specific questions when they seem useful. I also provide my thoughts on the situation, but they ought not be construed as answers. After discussants have been through the case studies, I hope they can look at a dispute over public documents in private hands and quickly see the perspectives both sides bring to it and then how each might individually address it.

Disclosure

In the spirit of full disclosure, I should reveal my affiliations. I started my career in the world of historical manuscripts working in the Research Center of the Henry Sheldon Museum, a local history museum and collecting repository in Middlebury, Vermont. I moved briefly to the Vermont State Archives and eventually to the Special Collections Department at the University of Vermont. Today, I make my living educating incipient archivists at Louisiana State University's School of Library and Information Science (SLIS). As the adviser to all the aspiring archivists at SLIS, and as the professor in most of their archives classes, I make a point of reading the archives literature and drawing my students into the relevant topics they will face in their careers. I believe absolutely in the archival function,[9] and I care deeply about the world of archives and collecting repositories.

In 2001, I married David R. Chesnutt, who has been the publisher of many of the Manuscript Society's publications and the editor of its journal since 1980. In the years since we married, I have come to know the leadership and many of the members of the Manuscript Society. I find them good company. For that reason, I found the characterization of them in the 2009 SAA meeting disturbing. While I recognized that not all collectors and dealers act ethically, or even legally, most I know are honorable people. I was deeply troubled that people I like and admire in two different worlds could be so at odds with each other's perspective on the world. But, I had to admit that I actually knew more about the archivists' position than that of the Manuscript Society members.

That has changed; I have read extensively in the history and psychology of collecting and the history of the care of public documents in the United States. I think I have reached the point where I can argue both sides of a case, and I'm sympathetic to both. In this book, I have attempted to present both sides sympathetically, so the reader can work with the cases thinking well of both sides; that mind-set makes coming to a decision much harder.

Notes

1. David Lowenthal, *The Past is a Foreign Country* (Cambridge: Cambridge University Press, 1985); David Lowenthal, *The Heritage Crusade and the Spoils of History* (Cambridge: Cambridge University Press, 1998).

2. Ellen Gamerman, "The Case of the Disappearing Documents," *Wall Street Journal*, Sept. 30, 2011, http://online.wsj.com/article/SB10001424052970204422404576596873383476078.html?mod=ITP_fridayjournal_0 (Sept. 30, 2011).

3. Ernst Posner, "Archival Administration in the United States," in *Archives and the Public Interest,* ed. Ernst Posner and Kenneth W. Munden (Washington, DC: Public Affairs Press, 1967), 115.

4. Posner, "Archival Administration," 115.

5. Randolph G. Adams, "The Character and Extent of Fugitive Archival Material," *American Archivist* 2 (April 1939): 85–96.

6. Richard Maass, "Arguments Heard in the Clark Case," *Manuscripts* 8:2 (Winter 1956): 113–116; Paul. V. Lutz, "Government Loses Suit for Documents," *Manuscripts* 19:4 (Fall 1967): 9–11.

7. Robert F. Metzdorf, "Lewis and Clark I: A Librarian's Point of View," *Manuscripts* 9:4 (Fall 1957): 226–230; Burt Griffin, "Lewis and Clark II: A Legal Analysis," *Manuscripts* 10:1 (Winter 1958): 64–67, 72.

8. Edmund Berkeley, Jr., "The Language of Autograph Collecting," in Edmund Berkeley, Jr., Herbert E. Klingelhofer, and Kenneth Rendell, eds., *Autographs and Manuscripts: A Collector's Manual* (New York: Charles Scribner's Sons, 1978), 53–62.

9. International Council of Archivists (ICA) defines the archival function as "that group of related activities contributing to, and necessary for...identifying, safeguarding and preserving archival records, and ensuring that such records are accessible and understandable." ICA Committee on Electronic Records, *Guidelines for Managing Electronic Records from an Archival Perspective*, ICA Study 8 (February 1997): 24, http://www.ica.org/en/node/30019 (July 6, 2008).

Chapter 1

American Archival Practice

> *"It may not be surprising that a newly independent people were too busy making history to pay adequate attention to the preservation of that history."*[1]

In a 2011 article in the *Wall Street Journal* explaining the operation of a spectacularly successful thief the FBI had apprehended that year, the reporter wrote: "The overall auction market for rare American historical documents totals $30 million to $50 million annually, with roughly 5,000 to 8,000 pieces sold per year, says Selby Kiffer, Sotheby's senior international specialist for books and manuscripts."[2] Note that the figure reflects only auction sales, and does not include the value of those documents sold by private dealers in over-the-counter transactions—an equally lucrative market. Unfortunately, much of the material that generates so much money is archival—it came out of a government archives at one time or another.

What Makes a Record Archival?

At a 2009 meeting with the Manuscript Society board of trustees, David Haury, Pennsylvania State Archivist and then President of the Council of State Archivists (CoSA), explained what government archivists consider archival material. He started with what they do not consider as archival: those documents created by government bodies but intended for distribution to individual members or organizations in society, such as licenses, outgoing letters, deeds, commissions, and all similar documents. Rather, archival records include records documenting the granting of licenses, in-coming letters, indexes to deeds, records of commissions granted, and other documents created by a governmental body and intended for its own keeping. Haury stressed that government archives keep only about 2.5–3 percent of potential archival materials; they destroy the rest.[3]

The National Archives and Records Administration (NARA) provides the following examples of archival U.S. government documents to illustrate its point: "architectural drawings, certificates, charts, drawings, electronic historical documents, forms, legal documents, letters, maps, memos, motion picture films, photographs, plans, posters, and other documents created or acquired and kept by the President and his staff, Congress, and Federal governmental agency employees and contractors as part of their official Federal jobs." NARA also repeats Haury's point that government agencies routinely create many documents that go to people outside government, such as signed photographs or letters containing answers to questions posed by the public, and they do not regard those outgoing items as U.S. government records. NARA asserts that most of the time, one can easily identify a federal record by determining if the historical document was used by the White House or another federal office[4] because it will have some self-describing mark that alerts the viewer to that fact.

The problem of whether or not a document outside a government archives should go into one starts with history, of course; everything does. Today the federal government and each of the states has institutions, policies, procedures, and a culture in place to protect archival materials, but not in the past. Until the late nineteenth century in the United States, the definitions and laws so clearly defined in the fifth chapter of this book did not exist as they do now, nor did a governmental bureaucracy to enforce them exist at any level. The following section on the history of archives in the United States traces the origin of the problems between today's documents collectors and government archivists.

Seventeenth- and Eighteenth-Century Record-Keeping Practices

From the beginning of European settlement in the New World, people wrote "histories" of their experiences. One historian saw the earliest British works about North American settlements—those written before 1660—driven by three basic motives: 1) a desire to promote settlement (John Smith), 2) a desire to prove the moral and political legitimacy of the powerful (John Winthrop), or 3) a desire to disprove the moral and political legitimacy of the powerful (Edward Johnson). The modern concept of scientific neutrality as essential to the credibility of any history did not exist until the nineteenth century. Seventeenth-century "historians" of New England wrote from personal experience; they did not rely on primary documents to support their points of view and they omitted much that did not support their point of view.[5]

After the English Civil War and the Restoration (1641–1661), and after the first generation of North American settlers had largely died off, the Stuarts returned to the English thrown seeking to consolidate Royal power and expand English colonies in North America. To consolidate Royal control over the North American colonies, the King challenged the political legitimacy of colonial leaders and the rights to self-governance granted by the early charters. Resistance grew among the colonists—especially in New England. Defenders of colonial rights and the original Royal Charters realized they could no longer rely simply on memory and personal experience as a form of defense. They found themselves in need of historical records to support their claims. To protect their history, they collected, and then hid, documents that granted them their rights lest the British destroy the documents and revoke the rights and privileges guaranteed by them.[6]

English settlers, and most others in North America, left a country that did not have an archival tradition, and so they brought none with them and had none to fall back on. Europe generally followed a tradition in which records stayed in the possession of their creators. The modern concept of a national archives emerged from the French Revolution,[7] and by then the United States had become an independent nation. In Europe, government archives emerged as institutions in the nineteenth century, but not in the United States until the early twentieth century.

Even so, colonial governments sensed they should care for their records, especially court records. Legislation on the matter dates back as far as 1638 in Maryland and 1639 in Massachusetts.[8] Evidence suggests that Virginia even built a fire-proof public records repository in Williamsburg.[9] However, officials followed and enforced the laws unevenly. Legislative journals and the acts passed by legislative bodies confirm a picture of losses and of negligence. Public records faced chemicals, extreme cold, extreme heat and humidity, water, mold, insects, animals, and theft. The inherently inadequate physical protection provided for the records exacerbated the impact of colonial officials who had little concern about preserving or providing access to historical records.[10] Burnette refers to "an amiable laxity of official conduct" by colonial officials with "little concerned about preserving, and having access to, records of past action."[11] About a third of all records became victims of fire.[12]

Given the dearth of archives and libraries in the eighteenth century, people concerned about historical documents collected materials themselves, often for their own use. One of them, Thomas Prince, 1687–1758, a Boston clergyman, voraciously collected documents and meticulously researched *A Chronological History of New England, in the Form of Annals*. In 1736, he published the first volume, covering settlement up to 1630. His second volume brought the chronology to 1633, but by then his financial support had run out, and he could publish no more. After his death, Prince's collection, stored in the tower of the Old South Church in Boston, suffered from poor protection from the elements. When the British occupied the Old South Church during the Revolutionary War, they destroyed much of what neglect had not.[13]

Other valuable collections fell victim to the political differences of opinion of the time. For instance, Massachusetts Governor Thomas Hutchinson had amassed documents related to Massachusetts's colonial period with plans of writing a history of the Massachusetts Bay Colony. In 1769, during the Stamp Act protests, a mob attacked Hutchinson's house and scattered his papers in the streets of Boston.[14] Similarly in an act of vengeance, a mob burned many of New Hampshire Governor John Wentworth's manuscripts.[15]

Nineteenth- and Early Twentieth-Century Record-Keeping Practices

Federal Government

The secretary to the Continental Congress, Charles Thomson, functioned for 15 years as records manager and archivist of the Continental Congress and the federal government under the Articles of Confederation.[16] In keeping with the traditions of the time, the records stayed with Thomson. When Washington became President, however, Thomson turned over all of the Continental and Confederation records in his care to the administration, which placed them in the care of the Department of State. Until 1903, the Department of State retained possession of the nucleus of the national archives, including the journal of the Continental Congress, diplomatic correspondence before 1789, and the originals of the Declaration of Independence and the Constitution.[17] Thomson had watched over the Continental Congress and Confederation records so protectively that today we have a much more complete record of that era than we have of the first few Congresses under the Constitution.[18]

By the beginning of the nineteenth century, the federal government and 16 states had established themselves as functioning governments. In addition, because of the admission of Vermont in 1791, Kentucky in 1792, and Tennessee in 1796, the federal government had developed a process for adding states to its number. All the governing bodies had laws on the books about the disposition of public records, but they had poor, if any, enforcement of those laws. The records got so little care that an 1810 Congressional "Committee to Inquire into the State of the Ancient Public Records and Archives of the United States" reported that the early records "were in a state of great disorder and exposure; and in a situation neither safe nor convenient nor honorable to the nation."[19] In an era when all manufactured heat came from a multitude of open fireplaces and other forms of combustion, records faced serious dangers just being indoors. The committee recommended that Congress make space for them in fireproof rooms. Unfortunately, the crisis created by the burning of Washington in 1814 ended that effort.[20]

The authorization for the Department of War stipulated that military records of conquered governments should go into its care. Likewise the Department of the Treasury had the authority to keep its own records.[21] In 1800 and 1801, serious fires destroyed large portions of the records of both the Departments of War and the Treasury. More federal records burned in 1814 and 1833. According to J. Franklin Jameson, a founder of the American Historical Association who also spearheaded the creation of the National Archives, 254 fires occurred in federal offices between 1833 and 1915.[22]

On February 6, 1853, Congress passed an act making it illegal to destroy any federal records. The Civil War created an especially records-intensive era, but federal offices, flooded with records, had no authority to dispose of any of them.[23] Vast quantities of valueless records hindered the transaction of business. Further, the lack of care in arranging and storing records made those that had value nearly impossible to find.[24] "By the 1870's many Government office buildings in Washington were literally jammed with records." Bulging files "containing applications for positions, letters of transmittal, monthly personal reports of officers, records pertaining to changes of station or duty, applications of soldiers for discharge or remission of their court-martial sentences, and vast quantities of other material of transitory value"[25] clogged War Department offices. President Hayes established a commission to study the security of Washington's government buildings against fire, and in 1877, he sent its report to Congress. The report addressed the problem of the large quantity of burnable old records, but it rejected the suggestion that many had no value and should be destroyed. As the President wrote, "Every paper worthy at any time to be recorded and placed in the public files may be of value at some future time, either in a historical, biographical, or pecuniary way, to the citizen or the nation."[26] The Commission recommended a fireproof building.[27]

Public records faced perils other than fire. Officials frequently failed to turn records over to successors when their terms expired, and many official records went from the office of origin into private hands. Officials often did not draw a the line between institutional archives and personal papers, especially in those cases where the official worked out of what we would now call a home office.[28] When others, frequently family members, attempted to separate public records from private papers after the death of the official who mingled them, they lacked an understanding of the records' context and thus the importance of their content. For instance, when the unpopular colonial governor of Massachusetts, Thomas Hutchinson, fled Boston in 1774, a mob scattered his papers in the street; someone gathered them up, public records and private papers alike. The official records automatically became the property of the Commonwealth as the government that succeeded the British, and claim to the private papers came open to question. In 1821, Alden Bradford, Secretary of the Commonwealth and a historical writer, had both the official records and the personal papers. He segregated the official from the unofficial and, with the approval of the sitting governor, presented what he believed constituted the collection of personal papers to the Massachusetts Historical Society, keeping the public papers for the state to care for. A quarter of a century later, Bradford's successor, John G. Palfrey, also a historian, demanded the Historical Society return the "private" papers to the state.[29]

Until the middle of the twentieth century, retiring officials, especially executive branch officials, assumed that they owned the papers that reflected acts of their own initiative and responsibility. Official papers "which become 'archival astrays' by leaving office with their creator usually constitute the historical 'cream' of the file."[30]

If an official did leave materials behind, they might later appear in the papers of his successor. Sir Henry Clinton served as Commander-in-Chief for North

America between 1778 and 1782, replaced by Sir Guy Carleton, 1782–1783. When Clinton left office, he skimmed off some of the cream, but not all. The papers of his successor, Carleton, include a large amount of material Clinton had left behind.[31] As a result, both the Clinton papers in the William L. Clements Library, at the University of Michigan, and the papers of Sir Guy Carleton in the John D. Rockefeller Jr. Library, at Colonial Williamsburg, hold Clinton's correspondence and related papers from the British Army Headquarters in New York City during the War for Independence. Eventually legislation and records retention schedules cleaned up the confusion of who owned what records and how long government departments should hold their records, but those mechanisms didn't become common until the latter half of the twentieth century.[32]

State Government

After the Revolution, patriotic fervor stimulated an interest in history and historical sources, but that interest did not spur state governments to provide systematic care for public records. Following European tradition, most of the older records stayed in the custody of the agencies that accumulated them.[33] "No state provided methodical concentration of its archives in a single, separately-administered depository."[34] As a result, no state was able to preserve complete files of their own records, either in print or manuscript form.

Over time, officials deliberately destroyed some of the records. Some records just disappeared. Some wound up as possessions of other states or the national government. "Many early Maryland documents apparently disappeared in connection with the research of historian John Thomas Scharf and others went into the collections of Peter Force and Jared Sparks." The Library of Congress acquired many New Hampshire documents when it purchased the private library of Peter Force in 1867. "In Georgia, the volumes of colonial records that had been transcribed in London at state expense were lent in 1887 to Professor Henry Anselm Scomp for use in his *King Alcohol in the Realm of King Cotton*; most of them were lost when fire destroyed his house."[35] Occasionally states made grand decrees about the management of their records,[36] but none pursued a systematic program in their management and preservation across time. Today archivists and collectors alike deplore the early treatment of public records, and both parties understand that the legacy of that treatment has produced the environment they work in today.

The Size of the Problem

Recall that in 1853, Congress passed an act making it illegal to destroy any federal records. As you read this section, bear in mind that one cubic foot holds 3,000 letter-sized sheets of paper and weighs approximately 30 pounds; 70 cubic feet weigh about one ton.[37]

Between 1789 and 1861, the federal government produced a total of about 100,000 cubic feet of records.[38] Between 1861 and 1916, that accumulation grew to about 1,031,000, with many of the older records kept in "alarming conditions."[39] By 1872 more than 7,000 cubic feet of records accumulated every year in the Treasury Building. The records displaced the desks of clerks and overflowed into corridors. Offices of the Department of the Interior and the Post Office Department had similar accumulations of almost unmanageable files.[40] In 1903 the problem of record keeping was so bad at the Department of State that Congress ordered it to send to the Library of Congress "any books, maps, or other material" not needed for current business. That order included a substantial portion of the Continental Congress records that the Washington Administration had received from Thomson.[41]

The New Deal of the 1930s produced about 3,500,000 cubic feet of records.[42] By July 1938, the accumulation of documents at the National Archives grew at the rate of 50,000 cubic feet per year.[43] World War II produced another 2,000,000 cubic feet annually. By then NARA had a fully functioning operation, and the demand on the archives reference service highlighted the problem of too great a mass of records. In response, NARA developed a rationale and process for destruction of lesser records to allow access to valuable ones. (Van Tassel, 28) In 1948, a commission appointed to study the issue reported that the federal government held 18,500,000 cubic feet of records, which cost $1.2 billion to make and keep. (Van Tassel, 28) In 1954, another commission reported that all departments of the government had a total of roughly 23,000,000 cubic feet of records—compared to 600,000 in Great Britain. (Van Tassel, 287) By the 1960s, records scheduled for permanent retention as archives accumulated at 200,000 cubic feet per year. (Van Tassel, 287)

The individual states had parallel experiences. In 1994, a Council of State Archivists survey revealed that the volume of records grew at a rate of just under 100,000 cubic feet per year for all state archives combined. That rate slowed between 1994 and 2004 to about 63,000 cubic feet per year, but in 2005 and 2006, it surpassed the earlier 100,000 cubic-feet-per-year rate.[44] In 2006, the combined holdings for all state archives amounted to more than 2.7 million cubic feet—up from just under 1.8 million a decade earlier .[45]

Solutions

The Public Archives Commission of the American Historical Association wrote in 1900 that "it may be doubted if in any country in the world archives of relatively so much value are so lightly regarded or carelessly kept." One advocate observed that "the condition of local archives in this country is such as to cause the United States to be classified...with the backward nations."[46] Those judgments reflect the result of widespread practice, but they mask efforts made by many, mostly history buffs, to institute better practices.

Preservation Through Publication

At the onset of the American Revolution, a New York bookseller named Ebenezer Hazard, 1744–1817, accepted an appointment from the Continental Congress as Surveyor General of the Post Office of the United States. In that capacity, he traveled extensively throughout the colonies. During those travels, he collected or copied many of the records that documented the areas he visited. He, among many, realized that a reasonable history of the Revolutionary War could not be written without evidence supplied by a wide variety of official and private documents from both sides of the conflict. In 1778, Hazard, backed by Thomas Jefferson, received support from the Continental Congress for the expense of collecting those documents. Hazard published two volumes of his *Historical Collections*, one in 1792 and another in 1794. They documented the settling of New England and the New England Confederation. However, he did not get the support he needed to publish his Revolutionary War materials, leaving him with an extensive collection of unpublished materials.[47]

The partial destruction of Thomas Prince's library of books, pamphlets, and manuscripts—a collection that had provided valuable materials for other writers of New England history—inspired the effort to preserve documents through the "multiplication of copies."[48] That principle manifested itself in the publication of *Collections of the Massachusetts Historical Society* in 1792. Between 1830 and 1860, Jared Sparks and Peter Force continued the tradition of preservation by publication at the federal level.[49] The states, however, generally didn't adopt the practice. Many wouldn't fund the effort, and many did not have the historic materials they needed to create a publication, although some mined British archives for copies of records they could use.

Pennsylvania proved an exception when it had Ebenezer Hazard's son, Samuel, edit the early papers of Pennsylvania.[50] Unfortunately, this "preservation by publication" effort, designed to preserve historical information, fostered an attitude in the minds of many that published copies made keeping and caring for the originals unnecessary.[51] Many of the Pennsylvania papers Samuel Hazard edited disappeared after publication.[52]

Private Historical Societies

"The first drudgery of settling new colonies is now pretty well over," wrote Benjamin Franklin in 1743, "and there are many in every province in circumstances that set them at ease, and afford leisure to cultivate the finer arts, and improve the common stock of knowledge."[53] Thus, he supported the founding of the American Philosophical Society Library as a center for research in the history of the sciences, medicine, and technology.[54]

The histories that Hazard and others championed as a way to solidify and spread the story of the success of America appeared largely as state histories celebrating local individuality and virtues. However, Jeremy Belknap, a Congregational minister in Dover, New Hampshire, saw the value of a history of the whole nation and proposed a repository to collect historical documents on a national scale. With the endorsement of New Hampshire Governor Thomas Wentworth, Belknap began collecting materials. Both men understood that New Hampshire could not sustain the effort Belknap had in mind, so he turned to Massachusetts. In 1794 the Commonwealth of Massachusetts issued a charter for the Massachusetts Historical Society, and Belknap, its corresponding secretary, began a program of aggressively soliciting materials from throughout New England.[55]

Other similar historical societies followed. While naming themselves after a local area, many sought to collect from a far wider region. The New York Historical Society, founded in 1804, benefitted from more generous state funding than most. In 1815, the American Philosophical Society created a Historical Committee. It functioned poorly, and in 1824, a group of Philadelphians founded the Historical Society of Pennsylvania to concentrate on promoting the role of Pennsylvania in the nation's history. Van Tassel argues that after the War of 1812, "when the resurgence of nationalism...threatened to subordinate all states to the nation," the societies "set about the task of championing their state's primacy in the nation."[56] The American Antiquarian Society, in Worcester, Massachusetts, founded in 1812 under the leadership of Dr. Isaiah Thomas, a printer, publisher, editor, and bookseller, came closest to becoming a national repository. It focused on printed materials and "curious and valuable productions in Art and Nature." Thomas involved leaders from all parts of the country.[57]

Despite all the collecting, the writing of a national history did not appeal to historians of the day. They preferred to write biographies. To make the new nation worthy of serving as a model for others to emulate, biographers depicted the lives of the founders in as positive a light as possible. History as a scientific discipline did not appear in the United States until 1876, and "during this period, historiography, and especially historical biography, was regarded as a method of moral teaching, as a conservator of the established pattern of society, and as a product of competition between proud localities."[58] Biographers' writing depended on collecting or copying documents, although many authors did not feel especially limited by the facts contained in those documents—the country needed heroes and the world needed examples to follow. (Van Tassel, 67–73) This view led to the collection and preservation of the private papers of many noted leaders to amplify the official records created by governments. Jeremy Belknap and Ebenezer Hazard led the pack of collectors.

Writers of local histories did not feel constrained by the facts either. The victory in the War of 1812 ignited a fire of national pride and inspired writers of textbooks of national history to promote an "American character." New England writers dominated the field and New England values "set the standard for patriotism...wherever the history of the United States was taught." (Van

Tassel, 91). In support of this rise of self-consciousness and pride, localities all over the country established local historical societies. Inspired by the Revolution, Massachusetts, New York, and Pennsylvania established historical societies. The victory in the Second War for Independence inspired Maine, 1820; Rhode Island, 1822; New Hampshire, 1823; Connecticut, 1825; and Vermont, 1838, to do likewise. Following established models, all set about collecting histories of their founding and the genius of their growth.

In the same era, historical societies appeared in territories that had not yet attained statehood. Tennessee, Ohio, Illinois, Indiana, and Michigan all established private societies that encouraged the collecting of the memoirs and memories of first settlers. The founders had a goal of eventually writing a history of the state when statehood appeared. (Van Tassel, 95–96) In the 1830s, southern states picked up the trend. Virginia led the way in 1831, followed by North Carolina in 1833, Louisiana, 1835; Arkansas, 1837; Kentucky, 1838; and Georgia, 1839. By 1860, all southern states had established historical societies. (Van Tassel, 98) Van Tassel summarized the growth of these repositories saying, "Between 1790 and 1820, only four historical societies were established; in the decade between 1820 and 1830, ten societies were founded; between 1830 and 1840, twelve societies were announced; and in the period 1840–1860, forty historical societies were organized." (Van Tassel, 100)

Few of these state and local historical societies have an unbroken history from then until now, but wherever they existed, they collected materials that then went to whatever successor organization followed them. Van Tassel points out that despite their focus on local history, they all "expressed a desire to collect government documents and manuscripts, church and school records, town and county records, Indian treaties, and 'antiquities, geological, and mineralogical specimens, geographical maps and information.' They proposed, in short, 'to gather every fact that [would] illustrate the manner of life, the style of living, the habits of thought, the motives of action—of every kind and class of people' in the state to which they devoted their attention." (Van Tassel, 100) As one might expect, where interests overlapped, the societies competed for material, and they judged their success by the amount of materials they held. Their governmental holdings included government documents, treaties, laws, legislative journals, and official correspondence.

In the 1830s and 1840s, the value placed on historical materials stimulated autograph collecting and a growing interest in genealogy. (Van Tassel, 103) Genealogists wanted a wide variety of public documents to trace roots back as far as possible: church records, ships' passenger lists, town charters and records listing important people, military records—anything that would prove lineage. Compilers and publishers of such records fed a hungry crowd.

Establishing State Archives

Until the 1870s, when the tenants of the German school of evidence-based history became accepted in the United States, those who wrote history based it on whatever they pleased and spun it to suit their purposes. In 1876, fresh from studying in Germany, Herbert Baxter Adams introduced the first "scientific" seminar in history at Johns Hopkins.[59] In most cases the force behind the movement for government archives came from professional historians who wanted some "systematic care of the archives of the United States and especially the archives of the states." To support their "scholarly concern for the availability of original source materials,"[60] they developed an organized voice through the American Historical Association (AHA), which they founded in 1884.

The AHA's annual report for 1900 contains the results of a survey of public archives in Connecticut, Indiana, Iowa, Massachusetts, Michigan, Nebraska, North Carolina, Pennsylvania, and Wisconsin. "The commission found widely divergent conditions: some states had considerable accumulations of records, others, very little; some took good care of them, others were guilty of total neglect."[61] The report called for active support of any efforts to improve the care of documents. The AHA continued to survey and publish the condition of public archives, exposing state inadequacies. Conditions started to change. States began to create commissions and departments to systematically care for the state's history. It was a state-by-state process and each state devised its own name, organization, and placement of the archives in the governmental structure. And so it remains today.

In 1938, with the National Archives only four years old and the Society of American Archivists (SAA) only two, Albert Ray Newsome, Head of the Department of History at the University of North Carolina, in his presidential address at the second annual meeting of the SAA, noted that the 48 states exercising exclusive jurisdiction over state and local archives have resulted in "a generation of uncorrelated, unsystematic experimentation," which has produced "a wide diversity of legislation, administration and achievement."[62] He based his remarks on a study of state legislation on the keeping of archival materials he had directed. His work revealed an overwhelming variety of programs overseen by an equally wide variety of custodians, many of whom had little if any interest in archives. (Newsome, 1–16)

All states had laws requiring that any person have access to the public archives at reasonable times under the supervision of the custodians. (Newsome, 12) Forty states had "general laws with prohibitions and penalties...for some or all of such abuses as malicious, willful or fraudulent altering, defacing, mutilating, removing, stealing, falsifying and destroying" public documents. (Newsome, 9) Thirty-four states had laws addressing the "refusal or neglect of any public official to deliver public records to his successor." The states varied widely in the details of how that delivery would be accomplished. (Newsome, 10)

Most states had suffered some loss to fire, some multiple times,[63] but only nine states required some sort of fireproof housing for archival records.[64] Thirty-five states had legal provisions "for the restoration of lost, missing or destroyed archives, usually through rerecording the original or a certified copy." (Newsome, 11)

Newsome found that 33 states had "official state agencies for the centralized administration of noncurrent state records." However, although the state archives had the mission of centralizing the management of noncurrent records, "usually the centralization of state and local archives is by permission, negotiation and persuasion rather than compulsion." (Newsome, 7) In nine states, effective control rested with a political official or department "whose archival interest and knowledge is accidental and secondary." (Newsome, 4–6)

Newsome also found problems with the way creators and administrators handled records and that "no existing state public records law deals adequately with all archival problems." Only 15 attempted to define public archives. Eleven regulated the quality of the paper and ink used in the creation of public records; eight required permanent ink. Only ten states had some legislation to regulate the disposition of the archives of defunct or transferred offices or agencies. (Newsome, 11–12) Only four "have laws definitely requiring each public officer to make all records necessary to a full knowledge of the activities of his office and designating him as the legal custodian of the records." (Newsome, 8)

Twenty-one states had some provision for the destruction of public records. Newsome observed that "laws do not command universal obedience nor are they self-enforcing." (Newsome, 14) Only 11 states had directed authorities to examine and report on the condition of public archives and to supervise their administration and the enforcement of the public records laws. (Newsome, 15)

In the decades after Newsome's research, the development of state archives moved along in fits and starts. Not until the 1970s did the National Archives provide any systematic and material support to their maturation—a story covered in chapter 3.

Establishing Federal Archives

Although the concepts and institutions of archives go back as far as 2000 BC, the first modern archives, the Archivo General de Simancas, appeared in Spain in the fifteenth century. France established the Archives Nationales in 1789. In the 1800s, England organized a records commission to systematize the preservation and use of public documents when it established its Public Records Office in 1838.[65] These three colonial powers, Spain, France, and England, all introduced archival practices to their colonies, but England introduced them last. The United States had ceased being a colony in 1783 and did not receive that introduction.

During the Revolutionary War, Elbridge Gerry of Massachusetts "proposed in Congress that each state should designate an official to collect 'material'...of the period. The proposal was not acted on."[66] A law passed on April 28, 1810, provided for a federal archives to be housed in several fireproof depositories west of the President's House. Nothing came of it. For the next few decades "archival holdings of the Federal Government were decimated by fire, loss, and deliberate destruction."[67]

Again, recall that in 1853 Congress passed an act making it illegal to destroy any federal records. The Civil War made that practice a nightmare. In 1864, the Secretary of War set up the Archives Office of the War Department, which received the captured records of the Confederacy as well as Union Records.[68] General

Order Number 60 (April 1865) directed all Union field commanders to send all records, including captured Confederate records, to Washington.[69] Government workers systematically examined and organized the "Rebel Archives" as Secretary of War Edwin Stanton sought evidence of Jefferson Davis's involvement with the Lincoln assassination.[70]

Even before the Civil War ended, historians had begun to publish its history. After it ended, those wanting to write their regimental histories pressured both federal and state governments to publish the official records of that war so they would have access to them. Disregarding the pressure, the War Records Office made a policy of serving only those who came to it, and then, reluctantly. In 1874, Congress legislated the publication of the records of both sides of the war. Those publications inspired a new rash of regimental histories in the 1890s.[71] Likewise at the state level, the pressure from local troops and veterans' organizations and from regimental historians moved legislatures to collect and publish war documents, beginning with Pennsylvania in 1864.[72]

The rise of the modern state through the nineteenth century accompanied by the rise of a professional cohort of historians inspired most European countries to establish an archives by 1900. In doing so, European countries provided 1) a variety of models for national archives, 2) some indication of what establishing and managing a national archives entailed, and 3) a set of precedents for Americans, especially historians, to point to as they lobbied for a similar institution in the United States.

In the United States, the expansion of government and governmental records necessitated by the Civil War inspired voices to call for the disposal of useless records and the systematic protection of the valuable. By the 1870s, federal administrators could see the value of an institution for holding their non-current records. At the same time historians began to press for such an institution.

An 1877 fire at Department of the Interior increased the pressure. In 1877, 1878, and 1879 President Hayes recommended that Congress make provisions for the protection of public records, and the actual erection of an archives building seemed to move into the realm of the possible.[73] A fire in the War Department in 1880 prodded the Senate into passing a bill to support a "hall of records." An 1896 call for a Hall of Records resulted in plans delivered in 1898, but a bill to execute the plans did not get through both houses until 1912, despite an estimated 250 fires in Washington, DC, government buildings between 1873 and 1915.[74] Between 1881 and 1912 legislators introduced no less than 42 archives bills into the two Houses.[75] They all failed.

The AHA took up the cause of a National Archives, and much of the leadership that brought it into being came from it. The AHA envisioned a repository, like those in Europe, directed by scholars—not just a warehouse for old records. In 1895, as part of that pressure, the AHA established its first standing committee which set about creating a bibliography of guides to historical repositories in the United States and Canada. In 1899, supported by $5,000 from Congress, the AHA established its Public Archives Commission, which surveyed the "Perpetuation and Preservation of the Archives of Public Records of the Several States and Territories, of the United States."[76] The survey produced an impressive picture of archival holdings in America and a scathing indictment of their care. In addition, it regularly made a distinction between public records and private records.[77]

In 1913, Congress authorized the preparation of plans for an archives for the nation's records. WWI delayed the project and nothing happened until 1925 when President Coolidge supported a building to house and protect records of the government. In 1926, Congress authorized the acquisition of a site and the erection of a building. Groundbreaking in 1931; cornerstone laid in 1933; the agency that we now call the National Archives and Records Administration (NARA) appeared in 1934 as an independent agency, headed by a presidential appointee and staffed by professionals, with broad authority over governmental records, past, and present.[78]

However, while the archives staff had the right of inspection of all records everywhere within the federal government, the enabling legislation did not require agencies to cooperate. Agencies still had the authority to regulate their own arrangement, custody, use, and withdrawal of records, and many did, especially during war times.[79]

Further, even after the creation of NARA, destruction of records could only take place with consent of the Congress. Agencies forwarded lists of materials for destruction to the archives, which vetted it; the archives got permission from Congress. In the mid-1930s, the archivist calculated that agencies of the federal government created twice as much archival material between 1917 and 1930 as it had in the previous 127 years.[80]

In the 1930s, the Works Progress Administration hired 3,000 examiners to search the local offices of the federal government and inventory their holdings in a uniform way. The survey "revealed startling cases of misuse and neglect [such as] a depository housing inactive archives in one place being used at the same time as a pigeon-cote. Many kinds of valuable documents came to light, and historically important collections were saved from certain destruction. There resulted in many places an awakened sense of responsibility and archives consciousness among the clerks as...[materials] believed to be missing again became available."[81]

The establishment of the National Archives signaled a beginning. Over the next 30 years, it led in the development of a profession. Out of the profession came appraisal theory, processing guidelines, records retention schedules for managing large quantities of records, and the discipline of records management—a story I cover in chapter 3.

Initially NARA did not have jurisdiction over presidential papers. The presidential papers in the Library of Congress arrived there as a result of gifts or purchases from descendants of presidents.[82] Between 1834 and 1849, the government purchased large portions of the Washington Papers, the Madison

Papers, parts of the Jefferson and Hamilton Papers, and the Monroe Papers.[83] Franklin D. Roosevelt pioneered the concept of the Presidential Library when he established the Franklin D. Roosevelt Library at Hyde Park, New York, in 1939. Roosevelt's successors followed his example, but they did so as a personal decision. Not until the Watergate scandal of the early 1970s brought the importance of presidential papers to the fore did Congress pass the Presidential Record Act (978), which declared them public records.[84] While there have been dueling executive orders since then modifying the law, they argue over details, not the principle.[85]

For all that, government documents continue to go astray. Photocopiers make it possible for public officials to pocket an original document while distributing photocopies for officials to work on. Those government workers know that the photocopies assure no harm will come to history if they keep the originals of particularly interesting documents, such as "juicy" letters from well-known legislators and other celebrities, foreign and domestic. Such letters might never leave the possession of the public official who first handles them. The government has retention schedules and other regulations, of course, but their implementation depends on overworked mid- to lower-level administrators in offices with responsibilities that seem much more important.

One retired career federal official I spoke with worked for over 20 years in a variety of federal posts that exposed him to those practices. He told me he never knew of any administrative officers actually looking inside the file folders being retained according to a schedule. Administrators relied on the good faith of the officials responsible for working on the projects to which juicy documents related.[86]

Of course, practice differs from one department to another. My source assured me that the foreign affairs and defense jurisdictions carefully maintain the originals of highly classified documents plus those received officially from foreign governments. Likewise, treaties, diplomatic notes, and letters on sensitive topics received exceptional care—unless the President or well-connected presidential associates (including cabinet secretaries and other senior appointed officials) decide they want such documents in the presidential research libraries in their personal working files while they prepare their memoirs. While archival control of presidential and other high-level papers has grown more respected since the post-Watergate reforms instituted during and after the Carter administration, leakage of documents outside this controlled system still occurs, especially right before presidential elections and at the beginning of post-election transition periods.

Notes

1. H. G. Jones, *The Records of a Nation: Their Management, Preservation, and Use* (New York: Atheneum, 1969), 3.

2. Ellen Gamerman, "The Case of the Disappearing Documents," *Wall Street Journal*, Sept. 30, 2011. http://online.wsj.com/article/SB10001424052970204422404576596873383476078.html?mod=ITP_fridayjournal_0 (Sept. 30, 2011).

3. Archivists insist on destroying nonarchival records for a variety of reasons. If the state does not destroy them, it would have to mark every sheet as discarded to deter well-meaning citizens and dealers from returning them. If a state sold discarded records to dealers, it would have to keep records of those transactions and would still run the risk of having to deal with discarded materials coming back to it. When that happened, someone in the archives would have to figure out whether the returned material had gone estray or had been discarded. Either way, archivists see a lot of time and expense being wasted on nonarchival documents.

4. "Identifying U.S. Government Documents," http://www.archives.gov/research/recover/identifying-government-documents.html (May 25, 2011).

5. David D. Van Tassel. *Recording America's Past: An Interpretation of the Development of Historical Studies in America, 1607–1884* (Chicago: University of Chicago Press, 1960), 1–18. John Smith, *The Generall Historie of Virginia, New-England, and the Summer Isles*, 1624; John Winthrop, *The Journal of John Winthrop*, 1630; Edward Johnson, *The Wonder-Working Providence of Sion's Savior in New England 1628–1651*, 1653.

6. Connecticut's Charter Oak provides the most dramatic incident in this effort. http://www.ct.gov/ctportal/cwp/view.asp?a=885&q=246528 (Jan. 26, 2011).

7. Judith M. Panitch, "Liberty, Equality, Posterity? Some Archival Lessons from the Case of the French Revolution," *American Archivist* 59 (Winter 1996): 30–47.

8. Ernst Posner, *American State Archives* (Chicago: University of Chicago Press, 1964), 8 (Maryland) and 15 (Massachusetts).

9. James M. O'Toole and Richard J. Cox, *Understanding Archives and Manuscripts* (Chicago: Society of American Archivists, 2006), 54.

10. Ernst Posner. *American State Archives*, 8; Donald R. McCoy, "The Struggle to Establish a National Archives in the United States," in *Guardian of Heritage: Essays on the History of the National Archives*, ed. Timothy Walch (Washington, DC: National Archives and Records Administration, 1985), 1.

11. O. Lawrence Burnette, Jr., *Beneath the Footnote* (Madison: State Historical Society of Wisconsin, 1969), 45.

12. Burnette, *Beneath the Footnote*, 45.

13. Lucile M. Kane, " Manuscript Collecting," in *In Support of Clio: Essays in Memory of Herbert A. Keller*, ed. William B. Hesseltine and Donald R. McNeil (Madison: State Historical Society of Wisconsin, 1958), 29–48; H. G. Jones, *Historical Consciousness in the Early Republic* (Chapel Hill: North Caroliniana Society, 1995), 3.

14. Jones, *Historical Consciousness*, 3.

15. Kane, "Manuscript Collecting," 29–48.

16. Oliver W. Holmes, "Public Records—Who Knows What They Are?" *American Archivist* 23 (January 1960): 25.

17. Burnette, *Beneath the Footnote*, 7.

18. Jones, *The Records of a Nation*, 4.

19. Jones, *The Records of a Nation*, 5.

20. Donald R. McCoy, "The Struggle to Establish a National Archives in the United States," in *Guardian of Heritage: Essays on the History of the National Archives*, ed. Timothy Walch (Washington, DC: National Archives and Records Administration, 1985), 2.

21. Burnette, *Beneath the Footnote*, 8.

22. McCoy, "The Struggle to Establish a National Archives," 1.

23. Burnette, *Beneath the Footnote*, 9.

24. McCoy, "The Struggle to Establish a National Archives," 1.

25. Harold T. Pinkett. "Investigations of Federal Recordkeeping, 1887–1906," *American Archivist* 21 (April 1958): 164.

26. Burnette, *Beneath the Footnote*, 10.

27. G. Philip Bauer, "Public Archives in the United States" in *In Support of Clio: Essays in Memory of Herbert A. Keller*, ed. William B. Hesseltine and Donald R. McNeil (Madison: State Historical Society of Wisconsin, 1958), 64.

28. Winston Broadfoot, Director of the George Washington Flowers Memorial Collection of Southern Americana at Duke University, testified at a replevin trial that the town book of Wilmington, N.C., the town book of Brunswick, N.C., and a number of county records that have turned up in private attics. "State of North Carolina vs. B.C. West," *Manuscripts* 28:2 (Spring 1976): 131

29. Lester J Cappon, "Historical Manuscripts as Archives: Some Definitions and Their Application," *American Archivist* 19 (April 1956): 105–106.

30. Cappon, "Historical Manuscripts as Archives," 106.

31. Cappon, "Historical Manuscripts as Archives," 107.

32. J. Frank Cook, "'Private Papers' of Public Officials," *American Archivist* 38 (July 1975): 299–324, provides a review of the assumptions and debates that finally settled the issue.

33. Bauer, "Public Archives in the United States," 51.

34. Bauer, "Public Archives in the United States," 51.

35. Bauer, "Public Archives in the United States," 51.

36. In 1784, for instance, a committee of the New Jersey legislature recommended that the records of the secretary's office at Burlington shouldn't be moved to Trenton until the state put up a suitable building for them. Bauer, "Public Archives in the United States," 51.

37. Burnette, *Beneath the Footnote*, 287.

38. Burnette, *Beneath the Footnote*, 287.

39. McCoy, "The Struggle to Establish a National Archives," 2.

40. Pinkett, "Investigations of Federal Recordkeeping, 1887–1906," 164.

41. McCoy, "The Struggle to Establish a National Archives," 5.

42. Burnette, *Beneath the Footnote*," 287.

43. Van Tassel, *Recording America's Past*, 22.

44. Council of State Archivists, *The State of State Records: A Status Report on State Archives and Records Management Programs in the United States* (Iowa City: Council of State Archivists, 2007), 25.

45. Council of State Archivists, *The State of State Records*, tables 2.1, 2.2.

46. David L. Smiley. "The W.P.A. Historical Records Survey," in *In Support of Clio: Essays in Memory of Herbert A. Keller*, ed. William B. Hesseltine and Donald R. McNeil (Madison: State Historical Society of Wisconsin, 1958), 9.

47. Posner, *American State Archives*, 11. I can find no information on what became of Hazard's collection.

48. Van Tassel, *Recording America's Past*, 22.

49. Donald R. McCoy, *The National Archives: America's Ministry of Documents* (Chapel Hill: University of North Carolina Press, 1978), 4.

50. Roland M. Baumann, "Samuel Hazard: Editor and Archivist for the Keystone State," *Pennsylvania Magazine of History and Biography* 107, no. 2 (April 1983): 195–215.

51. Posner, *American State Archives*, 13

52. Bauman, "Samuel Hazard," 209–210.

53. American Philosophical Society, http://www.amphilsoc.org/about (Nov. 21, 2009).

54. American Philosophical Society, http://www.amphilsoc.org/about (Nov. 21, 2009).

55. Burnette, *Beneath the Footnote*, 134.

56. Van Tassel, *Recording America's Past*, 65.

57. "A Brief History of the American Antiquarian Society," http://www.americanantiquarian.org/briefhistory.htm (March 16, 2011).

58. Van Tassel, *Recording American's Past*, 75.

59. Posner, *American State Archives*, 17.

60. Posner, *American State Archives*, 16.

61. Posner, *American State Archives*, 19.

62. Albert Ray Newsome, "Uniform State Archival Legislation," *American Archivist* 2 (January 1939): 1.

63. Leslie W. Dunlap, *American Historical Societies, 1790–1860*. (Madison: Privately Printed, 1944), 58.

64. Newsome, "Uniform State Archival Legislation," 12.

65. Van Tassel, *Recording America's Past*, 105.

66. Jones, *Historical Consciousness*, 51.

67. Ernst Posner, "Archival Administration in the United States," in *Archives and the Public Interest*, ed. Ernst Posner and Kenneth W. Munden (Washington, DC: Public Affairs Press, 1967), 119.

68. Burnette, *Beneath the Footnote*, 8.

69. United States War Department, *The War of the Rebellion: A Compilation of the Official Records of the Union and Confederate Armies*. Series III, Vol. IV (Pasadena, CA: Historical Times, 1985), 1258–1259.

70. Burnette, *Beneath the Footnote*, 8.

71. Van Tassel, *Recording America's Past*, 149–153.

72. Van Tassel, *Recording America's Past*, 151.

73. Posner, "Archival Administration in the United States," 119.

74. Jones, *The Records of a Nation*, 6.

75. Posner, "Archival administration in the United States," 119.

76. Public Archives Commission of the American Historical Association, *Annual Report of the American Historical Association for the Year 1900: Vol. II: Report of the Public Archives* (Washington, DC: Government Printing Office, 1901), 16.

77. Posner, *American State Archives*, 19.

78. Donald R. McCoy, *The National Archives* (Chapel Hill: University of North Carolina Press, 1978), 9.

79. McCoy, *The National Archives*, 10.

80. Posner, "Archival Administration in the United States," 119.

81. Posner, "Archival administration in the United States," 128.

82. Cappon, "Historical Manuscripts as Archives," 106.

83. Fred Shelley, “Manuscripts in the Library of Congress: 1800–1900,” *American Archivist* 11 (January 1948): 6.

84. Not until 1986, however, did NARA get legislative control over all Presidential Libraries.

85. Presidential Records Act (PRA) of 1978, http://www.archives.gov/presidential-libraries/laws/1978-act.html (Feb. 6, 2011).

86. Personal conversation, Nov.15, 2010.

Chapter 2

Theft and Neglect

Given the laxness of local, state, and federal laws and the enforcement of those laws, it will come as no surprise that many public records simply disappeared as a result of theft, neglect, or deliberate disposal. To give some reality to that fairly abstract statement, I've collected here a sampling of the examples I found in print, which I have arranged in chronological order. I have no doubt they represent an extremely small proportion of the loss, but they provide good illustrations of how documents went estray of their keepers. After examples of garden variety theft and neglect, I examine the issue of the "spoils of war" as it has applied to American manuscripts.

Two other publications also contain astonishing stories of abuse and neglect of public documents. First, the American Historical Association (AHA), in its annual report for 1900, reported on the results of a survey of public archives in Connecticut, Indiana, Iowa, Massachusetts, Michigan, Nebraska, North Carolina, Pennsylvania, and Wisconsin.[1] As I quoted in chapter 1, "The commission found widely divergent conditions: some states had considerable accumulations of records, others, very little; some took good care of them, others were guilty of total neglect."[2] The bulk of the book details those conditions, especially those of total neglect.

Second, funded by the Council on Library Resources, Ernst Posner conducted a survey of state archival agencies between February 1962 and November 1963. He reported, state-by-state, the history of archival care and the then-current status. The background statements do not reflect well on many states.[3] Compared to those two studies, what I recount below barely touches the surface of the problem.

In the Nineteenth Century

☞ Librarians and friends of scholarship in Congress proposed in 1822 that parts or all of the government's unprinted records be turned over to the Library of Congress, hoping that it would take better care of them and make them more accessible. Nothing happened. The same idea appeared repeatedly throughout the nineteenth century. "Inaction on these proposals was caused not by any concern that the Library would not properly care for the archives, or in any hope that such a splendid organization as now exists for the care of archives would one day be created, but rather from a complete disregard and total lack of concern by officialdom of what might happen to the archives of the United States."[4]

☞ Representative Edward Everett proposed in 1827 that the government obtain copies of foreign archives relating to America, especially those of Britain. The proposal failed. He also urged the purchase of the manuscripts and printed books of U.S. Consul at Valencia Obadiah Rich. Rich's collection included many original unpublished documents relating to the history of America. Congress took no action and James Lenox eventually acquired the Rich collection.[5]

☞ In 1828, a bill to copy English records did not pass. The proposal for copying or calendaring of English archives reappeared again three decades later but again failed passage. "This large project had to wait many years before effectively begun, and then to depend upon support other than governmental."[6]

☞ In 1850, Congress debated whether to appropriate sufficient funds to purchase the original manuscript of Washington's Farewell Address. Senator Andrew Johnson of Tennessee ridiculed the idea by wondering whether the deal should include the pen with which Washington used to write it and the type and the printing press that printed it. The debate went on so long that the very day Congress passed the appropriation a private collector bought the manuscript.[7]

☞ In the winter of 1861, Dr. Thomas Addis Emmet noticed a driver on Pennsylvania Avenue in Washington, DC, hauling barrels of documents. The driver told Dr. Emmet that he had orders to dump them into the Potomac River. Emmet took a handful, which he later discovered were letters by Washington, Jefferson, Hancock, and others of the Founding Era. He watched with dismay "as the long line of sleighs…moved toward the river." He went to the Capitol and learned that the papers came from storage areas in the building needed to create kitchens to feed the thousands of soldiers arriving in Washington. "Under the great front square [of the Capitol] were vast chambers and vaults, lined with shelves that were stacked high with the original manuscript records of the Colonial and Revolutionary periods. The Army appropriated these rooms to install temporary ovens for the baking of bread, and the papers, haphazardly crammed into hogsheads, were cleared out for what was considered, according to military efficiency, the most practical destination—the river."[8]

☞ The Archivist of North Carolina testified at the replevin trial of B.C. West[9] that during the Civil War the state government deliberately moved documents to county courthouses for safety. He then went on to say that as Sherman's army approached, the records were dispersed in Raleigh, though he claimed not to know they had been lost.[10]

In the Twentieth Century

☞ In 1907, the Barge Office sat on the Battery in New York. "Its attic was filled with records, and included...many documents signed by Washington, Jefferson, Madison, Adams, Monroe and other Presidents."[11] In addition there was a full range of forms one would expect of a government office and the extensive correspondence of the Collectors of the Port of New York. When they needed more space, government authorities sold the entire contents of the attic, about 140 tons, to a junk dealer to take to a pulp mill. Walter Benjamin, who had been a manuscript dealer for about 20 years, heard of the sale. He went to the Barge Office and found the junk dealer loading the papers into large wicker baskets and burlap bags. Benjamin rapidly looked at a sample of the papers and asked to buy them. "Only by promising to pay for the manuscripts item for item, rather than by pound, did he arrange that the junkman would send the greater portion of the papers to his office. For months afterward, the sifting-out process, which required careful examination of each paper, continued while each week new deliveries of baskets and bags were made." Benjamin describes this episode in an issue of his journal, *The Collector*,[12] claiming that this same period more than a dozen other custom houses in various parts of the country were cleaned out of the majority of their records.[13]

☞ General William Irvine, a distinguished General in the American Revolution, lived in Philadelphia. He had a large estate, which he willed to the State of Pennsylvania. When the state took over the entire property, it decided to preserve the main mansion, but had no interest in the caretaker's house, so they ordered it razed. Before they could raze it, they needed to clean it out. It so happened that all of Irvine's papers, letters of the signers of the Constitution, Abraham Baldwin, Jacob Broom, letters of Washington, of other people writing to General Irvine, were in that caretaker's house. The sßtate sent them all to the dump. A dealer came upon them, collected them, and offered them to Yale University. Yale had no interest since the papers did not relate either to Yale or Connecticut. Dr. James Babb, a librarian, suggested the dealer offer them to Mary Benjamin, another dealer. Benjamin bought them. Much of the collection went to the Historical Society of Pennsylvania. Ms. Benjamin wrote, "I feel it is my duty to offer things of that kind, to preserve them properly in an institution."[14]

☞ In an attic in abandoned house in Cincinnati, some boys found a box of letters Abraham Lincoln had written to his secretary, Thomas Tate. They took the box to a librarian, who suggested they get in touch with Mary Benjamin. She bought the letters and sold them to John D. Rockefeller, Jr., who presented them to Brown University.[15]

☞ "As late as 1919, the U.S. State Department reportedly disposed of thousands of presidential documents that took up too much space in the Executive Office Building. Some of these documents ended up on the open market and in the hands of collectors and dealers."[16]

☞ In the late 1930s some 40 tons of papers from the Philadelphia custom house were sold to various purchasers for a few hundred dollars. Congress had just passed an act that permitted the Archivist of the United States to make recommendations for the disposal of "useless papers." NARA sent a list of papers to be disposed of, all dated after 1910. The list arrived at the Philadelphia custom house office at an extremely busy time, and clerks were given only a few hours in which to execute the order. The clerks responsible for the checking and removal of the papers hurried through their task carelessly. Dr Julian P. Boyd, then Director of the Historical Society of Pennsylvania, attended the sale and bought some of the papers. He wrote that "they threw into one great mass practically everything they could lay their hands on, and I myself saw one document as early as 1743 in the mass of forty tons."[17]

☞ "Among American librarians and in the autograph and manuscript trade, it is generally known that a vast number of the papers of the War Department in Washington were discarded." Apparently the person who hauled them away did not burn them as ordered. As a result, many items have appeared at auctions and in dealers' catalogs many times over the decades since. Mary Benjamin claimed that institutions all over the country have absorbed them.[18]

☞ In 1963, the State of Connecticut closed its Wethersfield Prison after nearly 140 years of service. The prison building then served as a warehouse for old state records, many dated between 1775 and 1800. When the state decided to demolish the building, it ordered that a vast quantity of the records should go to a dump. Word of the planned dumping came to the attention of some antique dealers, who met the state's trucks at the landfill with pickup trucks and hauled away at least two pickup loads. "This is generally known at least among older collectors as the 'Wethersfield Prison dumping.'"[19]

☞ Edward Bomsey, a manuscripts dealer in the area of Washington, DC, observed that the state of Connecticut "tossed out an unbelievable number of things," including many bearing the autograph of William Williams, a signer of the Declaration of Independence. As a result, Bomsey claims, the many Williams autographs on the market have made his signature the least expensive of the Declaration signers.[20]

☞ For most of the twentieth century, theft at the Library of Congress remained largely unknown or unreported. One of the few known instances occurred in 1953 when a patron stole approximately ten manuscripts and tried to sell them to a dealer. The dealer reported the suspicious offer, and the authorities quickly apprehended the thief. "However, by the 1980s a rash of robberies came to light and resulted in congressional hearings and a major rethinking of security policies and practices."[21] The first of the robberies involved Charles Merrill Mount, who stole papers and letters worth in excess of $100,000 from both the Library of Congress and the National Archives. Again, a dealer Mount had contacted alerted agents of the Federal Bureau of Investigation, who arrested Mount on August 13,1987, as he attempted to sell 158 Civil War documents. With no actual eyewitnesses to the thefts, the Library of Congress had to prove ownership of the materials. Call slips and backup microfilm copies of the missing documents provided enough proof; the court convicted him of theft two years later and sentenced him to eight years in prison.[22]

The Mount case highlighted a human weakness in any repository's security system. Though not an employee, Mount's frequent use established him as a "regular" in the various reading rooms at the library and many employees considered him a rather privileged and trusted patron.[23]

Scott Petersen, a collector, occasional dealer, and intellectual property lawyer in Chicago, facilitated the return to the State of Illinois some "estrayed" original Lincoln warrants after he saw the inventories showing these specific items listed in the Illinois holdings in 1937. Later he noticed that the warrants had "disappeared" again and ended up for sale by a dealer.[24]

Spoils of War

☞ Lt. Col. David Thompson of the 82nd Ohio Infantry, while stationed at Fairfax Courthouse, retrieved Martha Washington's original will from being burned as the soldiers burned the courthouse papers to keep warm. His daughter sold it to J.P. Morgan.[25] That's one version of the story. Another version asserts that someone cut her will from the record book in Fairfax County while the war raged in that part of Virginia—likewise the will of George Mason, an author of the Bill of Rights, recorded in the same book.[26] The Fairfax County Court House sits near the Bull Run battlefield.[27]

In 1908, a friend of a prominent attorney in Fairfax County revealed that J.P. Morgan had it as part of his collection of wills.[28] A slightly different version says that around 1900, "F. W. Richardson, who had been the clerk of Fairfax county for 30 years began to receive letters from persons in New York asking if a clear title to the will of Martha Washington could be had. Mr. Richardson invariably responded that the original will of Martha Washington belonged to the people of Fairfax County and could not be legally disposed of by any one into whose possession it had fallen. Mr Richardson's mind is not clear on the names of those who wrote him."[29]

After Morgan died, the Daughters of the American Revolution (DAR) approached his son, J.P. Morgan, Jr., asking him to return Martha Washington's will. To their dismay, the son refused.[30] The DAR then prodded Fairfax County to take up the cause. In 1913, the Virginia legislature authorized the attorney general to sue Morgan in the United States Supreme Court.[31] In court Crandal Mackey, Commonwealth's Attorney General for Fairfax County, claimed the will was stolen property.[32] Morgan dismissed the demands to return it, saying that "the will was contraband of war—loot—and he had a right to keep it."[33] However, rather than argue his case to the Supreme Court, Morgan gave the document back.[34]

☞ "Many old court houses in the South were emptied of their contents during the Civil War, and it was said by contemporary witnesses that the path of the Union forces could be traced by following the old family papers strewn along the road."[35] The publicity given the case of Martha Washington's will stimulated a number of states to pass laws, modeled after the Massachusetts Public Records Act of 1897, forbidding the removal, defacement, or possession of any public record.[36]

☞ In testimony during the replevin trial of the B.C. West case in North Carolina, Naomi Chesson, employee of the Superior Court of Pasquotank County, North Carolina, for 34 years, testified that her county had stored a lot of court records in the bell tower of the courthouse. In 1961 the fire marshal ordered them removed. The Historical Society took some of them; others were destroyed. On the front of the courthouse a sign says, "Records dating from about 1700 were saved during the Federal occupation of the city (Elizabeth City) in 1862 by a brave Confederate and were hidden in a barn until the end of the war." She did not know the whereabouts of those records.[37]

☞ In testimony during the B.C. West case in North Carolina, Winston Broadfoot, Director of the George Washington Flowers Memorial Collection of Southern Americana at Duke University, cited the town book of Wilmington, North Carolina, the town book of Brunswick, North Carolina, and a number of county records that have turned up in private attics.[38]

"Spoils of war—loot," as J.P. Morgan, Jr., characterized it, no longer exists. The United States has joined a series of international agreements, which have made illegal the collecting of cultural or documentary materials from a war zone: 1) the Brussels Declaration (1874) declared that seizure of cultural treasure should be subject to court action; 2) the Hague Convention (1907) banned the looting of private papers and public cultural heritage institutions; Roerich Pact (1935) protects education, artistic, and cultural heritage institutions in times of war and peace. The Hague Convention (1954) superseded the Roerich Pact in protecting and regularizing the treatment of a people's cultural heritage during war. The UNESCO Convention (1970) made the clearest statement of them all about the complete protection combatants should provide one another's cultural heritage during time of war. The designation of items as "spoils of war" has a romantic ring to it, but under today's laws, Mr. Mackey, Virginia's Attorney General for Fairfax County, accurately described Martha Washington's will as "stolen property."[39]

Notes

1. Public Archives Commission of the American Historical Association, *Annual Report of the American Historical Association for the Year 1900: Vol. II: Report of the Public Archives* (Washington, DC: Government Printing Office, 1901).

2. Ernst Posner, *American State Archives* (Chicago: University of Chicago Press, 1964), 19.

3. Posner, *American State Archives.*

4. Fred Shelley, "Manuscripts in the Library of Congress: 1800–1900," *American Archivist* 11 (January 1948): 5.

5. Shelley, "Manuscripts in the Library of Congress," 5. James Lenox was bibliophile, philanthropist, and creator of the Lenox Library, which became part of the New York Public Library in 1895.

6. Shelley, "Manuscripts in the Library of Congress," 5.

7. Shelley, "Manuscripts in the Library of Congress," 6.

8. Mary A. Benjamin, *Autographs: A Key to Collecting* (New York: Bowker, 1946), 223.

9. See chapter 5, p. 55 for details.

10. "State of North Carolina vs. B.C. West," *Manuscripts* 28, no. 2 (Spring 1976): 118.

11. Walter Benjamin, *The Collector* 51 (February 1937), 38.

12. Benjamin, *The Collector* 51, 38.

13. Mary Benjamin, *Autographs*, 225–6.

14. "State of North Carolina vs. B.C. West," 125–26.

15. "State of North Carolina vs. B.C. West," 126.

16. Ellen Firsching Brown, "What Happens When Uncle Sam Comes Calling for Your Collection?" *Fine Books and Collections* (September/October 2008): 31.

17. Mary Benjamin, *Autographs*, 231–32; "State of North Carolina vs. B.C. West," 125.

18. Mary Benjamin, *Autographs*, 231.

19. Email to the author from dealer Joe Rubinfine with the subject line "Dumping of Ct. prison records" (Nov. 14, 2010).

20. Brown, "What Happens," 31–35.

21. Aaron D. Purcell, "Abstractions of Justice: The Library of Congress's Great Manuscripts Robbery, 1896–1897," *American Archivist* 62 (1999): 341.

22. Purcell, "Abstractions of Justice": 341.

23. Purcell, "Abstractions of Justice." The last four pages of the Purcell article contain brief accounts of 1990s thefts and Library of Congress's security efforts.

24. Email from Scott W. Petersen, January 4, 2006 with subject "Replevin."

25. O. Lawrence Burnette, Jr., *Beneath the Footnote: A Guide to the Use and Preservation of American Historical Sources* (Madison: State Historical Society of Wisconsin, 1969), 258.

26. "Will Sue J.P. Morgan for the Stolen Will of Martha Washington," *Columbus* [GA] *Daily Enquirer*, Jan. 8, 1914, 6.

27. "Want J.P. Morgan Sued for Relic," *New York Times*, Jan. 7, 1914, 2.

28. "Will Sue J.P. Morgan," 6.

29. "Will Sue J.P. Morgan," 6.

30. "Want J.P. Morgan Sued for Relic," 2.

31. "Will Sue J.P. Morgan," 6.

32. "Would Indict J.P. Morgan," *New York Times*, Jan. 8, 1914, 1.

33. "Will Sue J.P. Morgan," 6.

34. Brown, "What Happens," 31.

35. Mary Benjamin, *Autographs*, 231.

36. Burnette, *Beneath the Footnote*, 258.

37. "State of North Carolina vs. B.C. West," 132.

38. "State of North Carolina vs. B.C. West," 131.

39. Elena S. Danielson, *The Ethical Archivist* (Chicago: Society of American Archivists, 2010), 272–8.

Chapter 3

The Archival Profession

Like all human institutions, the archival profession in the United States has evolved over time. The previous chapter shows that governments had a general sense that they should keep public records for posterity, but no colonies or states had an archivist until the twentieth century. Even after the founding of the National Archives and Records Administration (NARA) and most state archives, archivists had no well-articulated theory about what to keep; no established policies or best practices on how to manage archival materials; and no formal educational programs for those responsible for the historical records. When NARA appeared in 1934, the American archival profession was hardly a profession at all, being "without a professional organization, a scholarly journal, a publications program, an educational structure, or a means for internal professional communication."[1]

In 1936, members of the founding generation of professional archivists in the United States, most of whom worked at NARA, established the Society of American Archivists (SAA) "to become the practical, self-help agency of archivists for the solution of their complex problems," to "strive to nationalize archival information and techniques," and "to encourage the development of a genuine archival profession in the United States."[2] The founders all knew from personal experience that "self-help" resources barely existed; they also knew that the profession they felt themselves part of did not really exist. For roughly the first decade of its existence, the SAA worked to establish itself as a viable volunteer organization. In 1940, it had only 247 members, most of them employees of NARA; 100 of them from the Washington, DC, area alone.[3] As state archives grew in number, their employees helped SAA membership expand, with Margaret Cross Norton of Illinois the most prominent spokesperson.[4]

Since most of the early SAA members had history degrees, they understood how a publications program could contribute to the stature of an organization and serve as a means for internal professional communication. Accordingly, in 1938 the SAA launched the *American Archivist* as its quarterly journal. Despite the practical nature of the society's mission, Theodore Calvin Pease, the first editor of its journal, saw his publication as a scholarly journal, eschewing articles on the technical aspects of administering archives. In 1945, Margaret Cross Norton became the editor and redirected the focus of the journal by filling it with articles on practical methods.[5]

Through the 1960s and 1970s, colleges and universities experienced tremendous growth and started establishing both their own institutional archives and a manuscript repository, usually called Special Collections and located in the library. In their Special Collections universities sought to document the history of the region they served. In their archives they sought to document their own history. Their archives also served to manage "the flood of paper that accompanied rapidly increasing enrollment, curricular expansion, and bureaucratic complexity."[6] Together these resources provided the primary materials for academic research needed by scholars on and off their campuses.

As a direct result of the growth of historical collections in academic settings, the 1960s and '70s saw unprecedented expansion in the SAA. In 1971, it had 1,000 members[7]; by the end of the '70s, membership stood at nearly 2,300. Regional associations began to develop, as did archives within businesses and religious organizations.[8] The majority of the new members in the SAA and regional organizations came from academic institutions.[9] These young and energetic archivists worked eagerly to establish their legitimacy as professionals in an academic environment that required them, if they wanted to advance in their careers, to serve actively in professional organizations and to publish research findings and theoretical perspectives on their profession. Before long, leadership in the SAA moved from the government archivists[10] to the academic archivists, and SAA programming began to reflect their perspectives. Academic archivists set out to enhance the professional status and public image of archivists. Further, "through the energy of these archivists, the governance of the SAA was democratized, its committee structure was reorganized, and a paid executive director was hired" in 1976.[11]

Also during the mid-1970s, major changes came to state archives. "A significant number of long-term state archivists retired...resulting in a generational turnover in the leadership of the state archives."[12] In 1974, government archivists formed their own organization, now called National Association of Government Archives and Records Administrators (NAGARA) to focus on their particular needs.[13] Less than a year later, the National Historical Publications and Records Commission (NHPRC), the grant-funding section of NARA, enacted regulations requiring each state, territory, and the District of Columbia to establish a State Historical Records Advisory Board (SHRAB) if it wanted to fully participate in the NHPRC grant program.[14] While members of the SHRABs represented the full range of repository types and historical records advocates, the regulations required that the state or territorial archivist chair it. To facilitate conversation among these state archivists, the NHPRC also created the organization now known as the Council of State Archivists (CoSA).[15] CoSA and NAGARA advocated for, and the NHPRC funded, the "advancement of sound practices and innovative programs for state government records."[16]

As part of this burst of organizational energy in the 1970s, the SAA increased its publications program. In 1973, it proposed the publication of a "comprehensive manual on the care and preservation of archival material."[17] That concept took shape as the Basic Manual Series of thirteen books on archival practice published between in 1977 and 1985.[18] Also in 1973, 35 years after it launched the *American Archivist*, SAA established the *SAA Newsletter*, renamed *Archival Outlook* in 1993. The newsletter provided a way to keep the membership in touch with the issues the council had on its agenda. *Archival Outlook* also provided a job placement service through its ads for job openings.

Archivists joining the SAA in the 1960s and 1970s "were interested in archival work as a permanent career, not just as a job,"[19] but education proved difficult to find. The first formal training in the United States appeared when NARA established the Modern Archives Institute (MAI) in the years following World War II. Its first participant attended in 1945, when the SAA had a membership of fewer than 300 members. The MAI became an established two-week program by 1950, when membership in SAA had grown to over 600.[20] In 1963, the SAA collaborated with NARA and initiated a series of one-day symposia on archives administration, conducted largely at NARA regional offices.[21] They followed that with a two-week course at Columbia University in 1965.

By 1968, eight universities offered courses in archival operations—most of them single one-semester courses.[22] Programs that awarded an archives specialization within an academic degree did not appear in American universities until the 1970s, when history departments and schools of library and information science (LIS) both began to address an underserved niche for history majors. The relatively young recipients of the GI Bill in the 1950s and early 1960s had filled the teaching jobs in the nation's history programs, so new graduates from history programs in the late 1960s and 1970s found few teaching jobs awaiting them. However, many colleges and universities across the country had newly developed Special Collections departments and needed archivists; new graduates from history programs quickly filled the need. "A 1970 SAA survey of archivists showed that 64 percent of the four hundred [respondents]...had a graduate degree, with one sixth holding the Ph.D."[23] A great debate ensued over whether archival education should come through history programs, LIS programs, or on-the-job training.[24] It symbolized to Frederic Miller "the lack of basic professional definition and common practice—let alone research and theory."[25] Both History Department and LIS advocates saw opportunities for their graduates, and both could argue for the centrality of their knowledge base.

A 1971 SAA survey found fifteen programs in the United States and Canada offering courses in archives management; eleven (73 percent) had appeared since 1965. Seven offered only a single course; eight offered two or more. The "advanced" courses tended to be hands-on experiences, not archival theory. The survey's report encouraged SAA to become more involved with archival education and it called for SAA to formulate guidelines and set standards for faculty qualifications, curriculum design, and instructional materials.

The SAA embraced the idea. In 1973, it compiled its first education directory, and supported the idea of developing masters- and doctoral-level curricula in existing programs rather than creating new ones. (Miller, 227–228) Over the next few years the SAA developed education guidelines, directories, and manuals. (Miller, 229) The 1976 Education Directory listed 17 schools with multi-course offerings and 23 with single courses. Practitioners taught most of them, focusing on the basic levels of practice. Miller sees the "Basic Manual Series," proposed in 1973, as representative of the knowledge conveyed in these graduate programs. No common body of practice, research studies, or theory had yet emerged. (Miller, 229) Regardless, in 1980, the Education Directory listed 47 multi-course programs in 32 states and the District of Columbia, compared with 17 such programs only four years earlier; all of them focused on practice. (Miller, 231, 236)

In 1981, when the Basic Manual Series had published about half its titles, Frank Burke, then Director of the NHPRC, took up the argument for more theoretical education. He suggested why no theory had appeared by arguing, "When we try to respond to the question 'Why?,' instead of to either 'What?' or 'How?,' we find that the hot, agitated atmosphere of the workplace, under the glare of the imperative for pragmatic solutions, is not only not conducive to the growth of theory, but patently destructive of it. *Theory can only grow in the cool and contemplative conditions of the cloister, i.e., in the classroom and its concomitant academic setting.*"[26] In other words, only with the growth of a serious academic curriculum in archival science—a curriculum that would produce research—would the profession develop a theoretical basis for its activities. Burke noted hopefully that "historians are in abundant supply. They are seeking alternatives to classroom careers. Academic history departments...are reaching for ways to prepare their students for the marketplace in adjunct fields: archives, museums, historical societies, etc."[27]

Through the 1980s, archival education moved away from practitioners moonlighting as college faculty. "As the 1970s closed, there were only seven full-time archival faculty (three in library science programs and four in history departments) in the United States. A decade later, the number of full-time archival faculty had risen to 21 (12 in LIS and 9 in history)."[28] These programs all resided in graduate programs and began to focus on theory as the basis for practice. As Turrini shows, in the 1980s LIS programs began to dominate the education of new archivists. A 2005 SAA study found that two-thirds of all new archivists come from LIS programs.[29]

Thus, out of the decade of the 1970s emerged five factors that have come together today to create the current situation in regard to replevin applied to manuscripts: 1) expansion of the SAA's publications program, which made archival theory and practice more widely available; 2) establishment of NAGARA as a professional organization specifically for government records issues; 3) establishment of SHRABs as a funnel for federal money into state and local archives programs; 4) establishment of CoSA as a forum for state archivists; and 5) establishment of graduate education in archives science, which subsequently has greatly clarified and advanced the theoretical basis for much that archivists do. The graduate education programs have produced a generation of archivists educated in the theory and practice of archival administration, replacing practitioners who had only on-the-job training and minimal theoretical basis for their activities.

The decades since the 1970s have seen the growth, clarification, and publication of archival theory and, with it, the emergence of a well-educated, theory-based cohort of professionals leading government archives. They have also seen the growth of regularly funded programs that promote the work of government archives. Today CoSA's programs include collecting and disseminating statistical information about state archives programs to support the archivists' political battles for funding and staffing. CoSA also serves as a clearing house for a wide variety of other issues state archives face, including the sale of public records.[30]

The Professionalization of State Archives

If the development of an archival profession required long and diligent work, that effort pales beside the challenges confronted by those attempting to establish and maintain an actual governmental archives.

As chapter 1 detailed, many colonial and state statutes established requirements for keeping government records but did not enable or enforce those requirements. While state offices had been accumulating records since colonial and territorial times, the lack of archival institutions resulted in great disparities in the records' physical condition and availability from state to state.

It took heavy pressure from the American Historical Association, exerted especially effectively in its alarming report on primary source materials in the United States, to move governments to action.[31] The report detailed the sometimes "total neglect" of public records in the states and "spurred 23 states to create central repositories for their archives by 1910."[32] Between 1935 and 1970, another wave of new state archives appeared, inspired by the establishment of NARA in 1934 and the records explosion caused by World War II. Seven states created an archives between 1935 and 1950, and 14 more before 1970. However, the fact that a state passed legislation establishing a state archives or records management program "did not guarantee that it would actually become a functioning part of state government. In some states, many years elapsed between the creation of a state archives in law and the provision of adequate appropriations, staff, and facilities."[33] Even today, state archives typically do not have the budget they need to do their job adequately.

As they established their archives, states placed them within the government structure in a way that made sense in the context and political reality of the time.

The first two, Mississippi and Alabama, created new independent agencies, but most assigned archival duties to an existing department, such as the state library, state historical society, or secretary of state's office. And so they remain today.[34] The quality of the support and management makes the difference between a good program and a weak one, regardless where the archives sits in state government. Further, archivists have come to substantial agreement on what makes a sound program for managing archival public records. It takes:

1) A solid foundation of records-related laws and regulation that allow the archives to define and enforce conditions needed to assure the survival of archival records into the future. That foundation includes a clear definition of what constitutes a record. In the mid-1980s, "only 24 [states] had detailed and explicit definitions, 16 had detailed but ambiguous definitions, 8 had only oblique or summary coverage, and 2 had no definitions at all."[35] Gradually that has changed. CoSA did a study in 2006 that found most state archives "have relatively strong legal authority in many key areas."[36]

2) Adequate resources—funding, people, and equipment—to exercise the authority they have. CoSA found in 2006 that all states spend less than one-tenth of 1 percent of total expenditures on archives and records programs; at least 13 allocate less than one-hundredth of 1 percent specifically to records. The report observed that "this raises the question of whether the level of expenditure is commensurate with the importance of this administrative function."[37]

3) Good descriptions of their holdings. Without good descriptions, researchers and archivists don't know what the archives holds, and archivists can't find what they have. Yet, a 2004 CoSA survey found that in 16 state archives "50% or more of their holdings were described at only the most basic level, e.g., title, dates, and quantity."[38] Across all the archives, 37% had their holdings described at this basic level, "41% at a midlevel that includes some information about creator and content, and about 19% at a detailed level."[39]

State archivists must work with the politics of their states. As Jones points out, every state archivist must wear, "in addition to an archivist's garb, the cloak of a diplomat, a politician, and, most of all, a missionary; for only through building personal and official relationships with members of the executive and legislative branches could he or she win the respect and funds necessary for the development of an adequate program."[40] Indeed, the CoSA report concludes that "perhaps the most significant trend behind all of this data is that state archives and records programs are working hard every day—both collectively and individually—to improve the management, preservation, and use of state government records."[41]

Archives as Cultural Heritage Institutions

In today's archival theory, a state's historical society serves as the repository of personal, family, and business collections, while the state archives documents the activities of its government. In today's archival theory, a historical society looks outward into the region its mandate would have it document, whereas state archives look inward to the state's governmental activities.[42] However, the state and national archives all pre-date that distinction, so government archives do more than just document the official activities of various governments. They also serve as historical societies and history museums.

Documents hold powerful symbolic significance. All literate cultures use documents to represent basic values they espouse. The United States government does not keep the original Declaration of Independence and United States Constitution in helium-filled vaults in a highly guarded sanctuary just so people needing to know what they say can go read them; millions of copies of the texts exist in thousands of different formats and places. The original documents stand as symbols of the nation we aspire to become, as well as a testimony to our esteem for the people who created those documents and this country.[43] Such documents-as-relics exist at all level of community everywhere. Every state reveres its founding documents, as does every city and town, whether the documents originated in the seventeenth century or the nineteenth.[44] Most revere correspondence or diaries written by the founding generation and subsequent luminaries. This attitude about documents exemplifies the attitude that led to the development of national and civic museums in the nineteenth century in both Europe and America, and today government archives serve some of the same functions as a national museum.

The 2007 CoSA report showed 39 of 49 states holding "non-government" records.[45] The websites of 24 of the states indicate that they still actively collect non-governmental papers; 20 indicate that they do not, while six did not address the issue. Of those that actively collect non-governmental records, the intensity of that collecting varies. Some seem to accept materials as a last resort, others indicate that they will actively seek materials within a defined collecting area. Some define that collecting area widely in terms of times and topics; others define it narrowly.

The reasons for this variation lie in history. As the states set up their archives, they implemented systems that differ as much as the states themselves. "A few state archives were established as independent agencies, other were assigned to state libraries, historical societies, secretaries of state, or other government agencies."[46] Those states that created their archives within the framework of a state library or historical society may not have clearly distinguished the administration and collecting policies for each unit. Other state archives accepted non-governmental material because no other state institution, such as a state library or state historical society, could or would. Many archivists find themselves in the situation described by Pennsylvania State Archivist David Haury: "We evaluate manuscripts based on their significance; are they primarily of statewide or local significance. If local, we work to find a local home for them." In the event they can't find a local home, the State Archives will take them in, because "if we don't save something, it doesn't matter whether the resource is a government record or a manuscript, it will be gone and lost forever."[47]

Although collecting of non-governmental records remains common in state archives, the trend toward separating a state's government archives and its collecting repository has grown. Today, the proportion of non-governmental records within state archives has diminished compared to the late twentieth century. "The Wisconsin Historical Society is now alone in having more private papers than state government records in its collections. In 1994 there were two such situations, with eight state archives in which one-third of their holdings were private."[48]

Clearly state archives belong to the collections-based institutions commonly referred to as cultural heritage institutions—like public and private historical societies, museums, and libraries. Such "collections-based institutions carefully choose objects of value and interest to some intended audience.[49] They preserve or stabilize these objects, arrange them, curate them, and present them to the public in reading rooms, galleries, and traveling exhibitions, as well as through various forms of surrogacy such as photographs and microfilm."[50] CoSA reports that "while some government archives give their main purpose as the support of the information needs of state government itself, most see themselves playing an important role in providing the public with access to government information."[51] Those archives reach out to the public by describing their holdings, both government and non-government, so the public knows what they have. Most make these descriptions available through printed materials and, increasingly, through the web. Then they assist a full range of researchers in identifying, understanding, and using archival records.[52] The biggest group of users of most state archives define themselves as genealogists, but other users include government officials, attorneys, surveyors, scholars, teachers, students, reporters, and avocational researchers.[53] Further, and very importantly, most state archives have some form of exhibit area in which they can show off their symbolically important material or just material they know the public will find captivating for some reason. A good exhibit creates much needed good public relations for the state archives program that put it on.

Evolution of Appraisal Theory

We can think of the creation, use, and disposition of a record as a "life cycle" that actually begins before a record comes into existence. When a government agency determines that it needs to create a type of record—a new set of forms, for instance, to allow citizens to comply with a new regulation—it includes in the creation process a directive as to what should become of that particular public record, i.e., who will administer it, who will store it. Typically a record's life cycle consists of three stages. A government agency 1) creates or receives a record in keeping with some aspect of its mandate. The agency then 2) maintains and actively uses the record, but gradually that use diminishes. Over time, the record goes from being considered active to inactive. Eventually there comes the time to 3) dispose of the record—through either destruction or transfer to an archives.

Step 3 has huge implications. If the legislation that sparked the creation of a document does not indicate what should become of the record eventually, the archivists must appraise it for its archival value. Appraisal for archival value, i.e., deciding what's worth keeping and why, bedevils archivists more than any other professional duty; if they make a wrong decision, they either leave a hole in the fabric of history or fill their shelves with materials of little historical value.[54] Appraisal sits at the center of everything else archivists do, for it establishes what they will have on their shelves and what their researchers have to work with. Therefore, the philosophical underpinnings for their decisions has led the profession to debate long and loudly over what archivists should keep and why.

The early keepers of American records all focused on their use to historians. John Jay, President of the second congress of the Continental Congress, wrote that he was "'carefully arranging the state papers of Congress' as primary source materials for future historians."[55] The political force that pushed the creation of a national archives came from the professional organization of historians. Overwhelmingly, the leaders in the development of the archives profession came from academic history programs and saw the role of archives as serving their needs.[56] When archival pioneers looked for materials to save, they looked at the information in the documents and its value to historians. However, the explosion in the numbers of public records that accompanied the growth of government throughout the nineteenth century made the job of isolating historically significant information very difficult. Archivists needed rules and methods for choosing, arranging, and describing historical documents.

In 1982, Frank Burke, in his contemplation of archival theory, posed the basic questions such theories must address, including: "What are the theoretical conceptions present in today's society that will color the acquisition or retention policies of archives, and how can archivists rise above their own social and intellectual environment? *Can we really foresee what segment of today's records will be needed by researchers of the future; and, if we cannot, then what countermeasures do we take as archivists to reduce the impact of our interpretive actions?*"[57]

Although England had a much longer historical record to wrestle with, when the Hayes Commission declared that any record ever created might have value, England's Public Record Office Act of 1877 allowed the Keeper of the Public Record "to destroy archives already in his custody and to refuse the receipt of records which he considered worthless," with the exception of documents dated before 1715; in 1898, the law rolled that date back to 1660. Along with this specific criterion of age, the laws warned against destroying "any documents which can reasonably be considered as of legal, historical, genealogical or antiquarian use or interest, or which give any important information not obtained elsewhere." This left a door wide open to any personal bias the keeper might have.[58]

In the nineteenth century, European archivists developed appraisal theories that looked to the office of origin and the value of the documents in it. In 1922, Sir Hilary Jenkinson, Deputy Keeper of the Public Record Office in England, published his *Manual of Archive Administration*, in which he asserted that the archivist should acquire those records that *the creators* thought most important. Similarly, through the 1930s and 1940s, Margaret Cross Norton, Archivist for Illinois, promoted the *administrative value* of archival materials, arguing that government archivists "should be intent upon building archives as an 'efficiency proposition,' dedicated to the 'scientific handling' of official records."[59] She took the position that "public records in a democracy belong to the people, that our government is made up of officials merely delegated to do for the people what the people cannot do effectively as individuals so that our officials do not own the records which they create but merely act as custodians of the records on behalf of the people."[60] Both Norton and Jenkinson argued that government archivists should document government activities without regard to historians' concerns.

Theodore R. Schellenberg of NARA, in clarifying appraisal policy for the staff at that institution, wrote of primary and secondary values in records. The primary value represented its value to the originating agency—as Jenkinson and Norton would argue—and its secondary values represented its value to the researcher—the historians' position.[61]

In the 1970s a flood of appraisal theory appeared.[62] In the mid-1980s, Julia Marks Young published a bibliography of the archival appraisal literature in which she annotated 121 books and articles. The earliest on the list had a publication date of 1940, two followed in 1946, but the overwhelming majority appeared in the 1970s and '80s.[63] The theories embrace a wide variety of methods, rationales, and names: Documentation Strategies,[64] the Black Box method,[65] the Minnesota method,[66] the Functional Analysis method,[67] the Record Continuum Theory,[68] and the Macro-Appraisal method,[69] among many others. Regardless, Burke's questions plague archivists still today. *"Can we really foresee what segment of today's records will be needed by researchers of the future; and, if we cannot, then what countermeasures do we take as archivists to reduce the impact of our interpretive actions?"*[70]

The discussion becomes more complicated as the volume of records grows and as governments create some of the their most important records electronically. Frank Boles provides a highly readable summary of the history and analysis of archival appraisal theory of the United States, and he concludes that the profession does not now, and may never have, a universally accepted theory on which to base appraisal.[71]

Whatever the appraisal theory in use, archivists and records managers have codified appraisal decisions into records retention schedules to keep the decisions consistent from year to year and administration to administration. NARA developed the discipline of records management in the 1940s, as it realized that agency records needed professional management during their active use for the archives to make any sense of them at all. Records retention schedules established what should happen to documents over time, how their disposition would occur, and who had the authority to carry it out. The vast majority of public records eventually go to some sort of recycling center. Through the use of both records retention schedules and disposition schedules, archivists and records managers identify and protect the critical records needed for current government operations and the 2 to 5 percent that belong in an archives.

Notes

1. William J. Maher, "Issues and Prospects for the National Archives," *Perspectives* (September 1999), http://www.historians.org/perspectives/issues/1999/9909/9909not2.cfm (Jan. 2, 2011).

2. J. Frank Cook, "The Blessings of Providence on an Association of Archivists," *American Archivist* 46 (Fall 1983): 378.

3. Cook, "The Blessings of Providence," 374–99; Nicholas C. Burckel, "The Society: From Birth to Maturity," *American Archivist* 61 (Spring 1998): 13–14.

4. Luke Gilliland-Swetland, "The Provenance of a Profession: The Permanence of the Public Archives and Historical Manuscripts Traditions in American Archival History," *American Archivist* 54 (Spring 1991): 167.

5. Cook, "The Blessings of Providence," 379.

6. Gilliland-Swetland, "The Provenance of a Profession," 169.

7. Cook, "The Blessings of Providence," 395.

8. Gerald Ham, "Report of the Secretary, 1969–70." *American Archivist* 34, no 1 (January 1971): 93; Cook. "The Blessings of Providence," 395.

9. Cook, "The Blessings of Providence," 394.

10. In 1956, the National Archives lost its independent agency status and became part of the General Services Administration. At that point it started to lose much of its leadership role in the Society of American Archivists. Gilliland-Swetland, "The Provenance of a Profession," 167.

11. Gilliland-Swetland, "The Provenance of a Profession," 170; Fredric M. Miller, "The SAA as Sisyphus: Education Since the 1960s," *American Archivist* 63 (Fall/Winter 2000): 229.

12. Council of State Archivists, *The State of State Records: A Status Report on State Archives and Records Management Programs in the United States* (Iowa City, Iowa: Council of State Archivists, 2007), 4. http://www.statearchivists.org/reports/2007ARMreport (April 15, 2011).

13. Nicholas C. Burckel, "The Society: From Birth to Maturity," *American Archivist* 61 (Spring 1998): 17. NAGARA has a current membership of about 250.

14. "Brief history of NAGARA," http://www.nagara.org/displaycommon.cfm?an=1 (Jan. 5,2011).

15. "History of CoSA," http://www.statearchivists.org/about.htm#history (Jan. 5, 2011).

16. Council of State Archivists, *The State of State Records*, 4.

17. Ham, "Report of the Secretary, 1969–70," 94.

18. Richard J. Cox. "American Archival Literature: Expanding Horizons and Continuing Needs, 1901–1987," *American Archivist* 50 (Summer 1987): 312.

19. Cook, "The Blessings of Providence," 395.

20. "National Archives' Modern Archives Institute Receives Top Archival Award," http://www.archives.gov/press/press-releases/2006/nr06-135.html (April 1, 2011). Currently the Society of American Archivists has about 5,500 members.

21. Cook, "The Blessings of Providence," 395.

22. Fredric M. Miller, "The SAA as Sisyphus: Education Since the 1960s," *American Archivist* 63 (Fall/Winter 2000): 225–26.

23. Miller, "The SAA as Sisyphus," 227.

24. Trudy H. Peterson, Patrick M. Quinn, and Hugh A. Taylor, "Professional Archival Training," *American Archivist* 40 (July 1977): 315–20.

25. Miller, "The SAA as Sisyphus," 226.

26. Frank G. Burke, "The Future Course of Archival Theory in the United States," *American Archivist* 44 (Winter 1981): 42. Emphasis added.

27. Burke, "The Future Course of Archival Theory," 45.

28. Joseph M. Turrini, "The Historical Profession and Archival Education," *Perspectives* (May 2007), http://www.historians.org/perspectives/issues/2007/0705/0705vie2.cfm (April 1, 2011).

29. Society of American Archivists, "A*CENSUS," *American Archivist* 69 (Fall/Winter 2006): 406. http://www.archivists.org/a-census/ACENSUS-Final.pdf (May 1, 2011).

30. "Sales of Public Records," http://www.statearchivists.org/issues/publicrecords-sales/index.htm. (May 1, 2011).

31. Public Archives Commission of the American Historical Association, *Annual Report of the American Historical Association for the Year 1900: Vol. II: Report of the Public Archives* (Washington, DC: Government Printing Office, 1901).

32. Ernst Posner, *American State Archives* (Chicago: University of Chicago Press, 1964), 19, cited in Council of State Archivists, *The State of State Records*, 1.

33. Council of State Archivists, *The State of State Records*, 3.

34. Council of State Archivists, *The State of State Records*, 59 (table 1.9), 17 (maps 1 and 2).

35. George Bain, "State Archival Law: A Content Analysis," *American Archivist* 46 (Spring 1983): 164–167, cited in Council of State Archivists, *The State of State Records*, 19.

36. *Assessment of Emergency Preparedness in State Archives and Records Management Programs*, cited in Council of State Archivists, *The State of State Records*, 19.

37. Council of State Archivists, *The State of State Records*, 20.

38. Council of State Archivists, *The State of State Records*, 33.

39. Council of State Archivists, *The State of State Records*, 34.

40. H.G. Jones, "The Pink Elephant Revisited," *American Archivist* (Fall 1980): 481, quoted in Council of State Archivists, *The State of State Records*, 3.

41. Council of State Archivists, *The State of State Records*, 36.

42. Frank Boles. *Selecting and Appraising Archives and Manuscripts* (Chicago: Society of American Archivists, 2005), 44.

43. James O'Toole, "The Symbolic Significance of Archives," *American Archivist* 56 (1993): 234–55.

44. Susan Pearce, *On Collecting: An Investigation into Collecting in the European Tradition* (London: Routledge, 1995), 130–39.

45. Council of State Archivists, *The State of State Records*, 25.

46. Council of State Archivists, *The State of State Records*, 3.

47. David Haury, Pennsylvania State Archivist, email to the author, April 5, 2011.

48. Council of State Archivists, *The State of State Records*, 27.

49. "As budgets have been reduced or buildings become full, I understand some states have become less active in soliciting [manuscript] materials.... In our case we evaluate manuscripts based on their significance: are they primarily of statewide or local significance. If local, we work to find a local home for them. If statewide, we are still aggressive in pursuing them...because I feel strongly that it is valuable for researchers to have one stop researching in both government records and manuscripts. And if we don't save something, it doesn't matter whether the resource is a government record or a manuscript, it will be gone and lost forever." David Haury, Pennsylvania State Archivist, email to the author, April 5, 2011.

50. Liz Bishoff and Nancy Allen, *Business Planning for Cultural Heritage Institutions: A Framework and Resource Guide to Assist Cultural Heritage Institutions with Business Planning for Sustainability of Digital Asset Management Programs*, CLIR Report 124 (Washington, DC: Council on Library and Information Resources, January 2004), vi. http://www.clir.org/pubs/reports/pub124/pub124.pdf (April 24, 2011).

51. Council of State Archivists, *The State of State Records*, 10.

52. Council of State Archivists, *The State of State Records*, 10.

53. Council of State Archivists, *Profiles of State Archives and Records Management Programs* (Iowa City, Iowa: Council of State Archivists, 2007), 3–53. http://www.state-archivists.org/reports/2007-ARMreport/FY06-profiles.pdf (April 15, 2011).

54. Except for the implications of the cost of housing archival material, archival appraisal does not involve money.

55. H.G. Jones, *The Records of a Nation: Their Management, Preservation, and Use* (New York: Atheneum, 1969), 4.

56. Gillilland-Swetland, "The Provenance of a Profession," 164–65.

57. Burke, "The Future Course of Archival Theory," 43. Emphasis added.

58. Ole Kolsrud, "The Evolution of Basic Appraisal Principles—Some Comparative Observations," *American Archivist* 55 (Winter 1992): 27.

59. Gillilland-Swetland. "The Provenance of a Profession," 165.

60. Margaret Cross Norton, "Some Legal Aspects of Archives," *American Archivist* 8 (January 1945): 5.

61. Kolsrud, "The Evolution of Basic Appraisal Principles," 35.

62. Maynard Brichford, *Archives and Manuscripts: Appraisal and Accessioning* (Chicago: Society of American Archivists, 1977); Thomas Connors, "Appraising Public Television Programs: Toward an Interpretive and Comparative Evaluation Model," *American Archivist* 63 (Spring/Summer 2000): 163.

63. Julia Marks Young, "Annotated Bibliography on Appraisal," *American Archivist* 48 (Spring, 1985): 190–216.

64. Larry J. Hackman and Joan Warnow-Blewett, "The Documentation Strategy Process: A Model and a Case Study," *American Archivist* 50 (Winter 1987): 12–47.

65. Frank Boles and Julia Marks Young, "Exploring the Black Box: The Appraisal of University Administrative Records," *American Archivist* 48 (Spring 1985): 121–40.

66. Timothy Ericson, "At the Rim of Creative Dissatisfaction: Archivists and Acquisition Development,"*Archivaria* 33 (1991–92): 5–20.

67. Helen Willa Samuels, *Varsity Letters* (Metuchen, N.J., and London: Society of American Archivists and Scarecrow Press, 1992).

68. Frank Upward, "In Search of the Records Continuum in Ian Maclean's 'Australian Experience' Essays in Recordkeeping," in *The Records Continuum: Ian Maclean's and the Australian Archives First Fifty Years*, ed. Sue McKemmish and Michael Piggot (Clayton, Australia: Ancora Press, 1994), 110–30.

69. Terry Cook, "Mind Over Matter: Towards a New Theory of Archival Appraisal," in *The Archival Imagination: Essays in Honour of Hugh A. Taylor*, ed. Barbara L. Craig (Ottawa: Association of Canadian Archivists, 1992), 38–70.

70. Burke, "The Future Course of Archival Theory," 43. Emphasis added.

71. Frank Boles, "Muddied Waters and Conflicting Currents" and "The Big Picture," in *Selecting and Appraising Archives and Manuscripts* (Chicago: Society of American Archivists, 2005): 11–73.

Chapter 4

Collecting

"Collectors themselves—dedicated, serious, infatuated, beset—cannot explain or understand this often all-consuming drive, nor can they call a halt to their habit.... A detached observer often finds it difficult to understand the immense passion and overriding concern a collector can exhibit about such things as old maps or a rare coin or military ribbons."[1]

What is Collecting?

The human propensity for collecting has inspired a remarkably large body of literature. Topics on the subject of collecting range from history, sociological, psychological analysis of through "how to."[2] Collecting, while something we've all observed and may even do, may not seem a very deep topic, but it is. Therefore, if we want to develop an informed opinion about the dynamics in replevin cases, we must refine our understanding of the people involved and their motivations.

Susan Pearce, formerly a Professor of Museum Studies at the University of Leicester, England, defines collecting as "the gathering together and setting aside of selected objects."[3] She argues that we distinguish among collectors and hoarders, misers, and accumulators by ascribing to the collector a rational purpose that we may not see in the others. Pearce observed that "to collect is to gather objects belonging to a particular category the collector happens to fancy."[4] Psychologist Werner Muensterberger defines collecting as "the selecting, gathering, and keeping of objects of subjective value."[5] Both Pearce and Muensterberger make the point that the *collector* ascribes the real value to the collection, which others may or may not agree with.

Consumer behaviorist Russell Belk calculated that one in three Americans collects something, and that collecting constitutes a special type of consuming. Ordinary consumerism, he argues, involves items to which people develop fleeting attachments, e.g., clothes, homes, vehicles, sports equipment. Collecting involves strong attachments. Ordinary consumers acquire, use, and dispose of items. Collectors actively, selectively, and passionately acquire and own things removed from ordinary use. Unlike ordinary consumerism, collecting stays relatively immune to fashion's whims.

Pearce sees the selection process as "the heart of collecting."[6] In the selecting, the collector distinguishes his or her collection from all others. Belk does not discuss the selection process specifically, but he implies it in his observation that "collecting is an essentially spasmodic activity. Acquisition takes place over an extended period.... Pieces enter a collection now and then as the collector is prompted to collect them, and the collection gradually gathers size, scope and momentum as time goes by."[7]

Muensterberger notes that "in some instances collecting can become an all-consuming passion...to the point where it can affect a person's life and become *the* paramount concern in [the collector's] pursuit, overshadowing all else: work, family, social obligations and responsibilities." Muensterberger then alludes to "numerous cases in which moral standards, legal considerations, and societal taboos have been disregarded in the passion to collect."[8] This passion, and the literature about it, applies to both people and institutions. After all, the New York Historical Society nearly went under because it couldn't control its collecting and the costs incurred in the process.[9]

Who Collects?

People of all ages, all cultures, all levels of wealth collect. Pearce finds that collecting habits and taste closely reflect most generalizations made about class. However, regardless of class, women tend to collect like other women, and men, like other men.[10] That said, Muensterberger observed that "there is...a distinctly individual and often wide disparity in the private incentives that motivate collectors."[11]

Public and private collecting institutions reflect and cater to the diversity of interests of the people who establish, run, and patronize them. Somewhere, someone has created a museum or hall of fame that will honor virtually any aspect of life anyone can think of. Every museum has a research collection on its topic, and that research collection includes historical documents.

What Do They Collect?

Everything. Somewhere, someone collects anything created by people or nature, but this book focuses on collectors and collectibles in the document world. People who collect manuscripts specialize within that world. They may focus on a genre of document, such as personal correspondence, signed financial papers, or government commissions. They may collect the work of individual people ranging from great heroes and heroines debased villains. They may collect categories of people, such as American Presidents or First Ladies, nineteenth-century English poets, American astronauts, etc. They may focus on an era or activity or place, such as nineteenth-century transportation, or a particular war, or their obscure hometown. Many combine people, places, events, and professions to become collectors of autographs of supreme court judges or correspondence about the gold rush in Alaska, or blue prints of nineteenth-century railroad bridges. Collectors have no rules they must follow besides their own interests and their financial ability to support their passion.

Archivists—government-supported collectors of public documents—do not appear to have much personal latitude in their collections; their collecting must reflect the legislation that created the archives and authorized their activities. Most archivists have some professional discretion, especially those in archives that collect non-governmental materials. Government archivists typically collect according to an appraisal theory, the traditions of their institutions, the mandates in the legislation that created and manages them, the political environment they work in, and, harking back to the 1898 directive to the British Keeper of the Public Record, their own instincts for what their archives should hold. Their instincts come from their training, their professional experience, and their interest in history.

Who Collects Documents?

According to Kenneth Rendell, until the second half of the twentieth century, only scholars and serious collectors sought historical materials. "Prices were low, large numbers of letters and documents were available, and most university and public libraries as well as historical societies had special collections divisions that were very active in locating and purchasing historical letters."[12] From the mid-1950s through the 1980s, institutions acquired an enormous number of historical letters and documents, so that by the mid-1990s, Rendell asserted that "relatively few collections or major correspondences...remain in private hands."[13]

In Rendell's experience, the private manuscript collector is fairly well read, frequently an entrepreneur, a decision maker, with a strong interest in the people and events that shaped our culture and the world. Many collect in areas that relate to their professions, but the majority collect in the areas in which they read. "What [all collectors] have in common is the respect for and interest in the genius and accomplishments of others."[14]

The general affluence in society as a whole during the second half of the twentieth century has democratized manuscript collecting in many ways, but "there still is an upscale and male bias among collectors." Because collecting historical documents requires discretionary money, the poor do not become document collectors. As Belk points out, since old documents don't serve any practical function, "they remain a luxury even in an affluent society."[15]

Much of the above about individual collectors applies to archivists. Many have multiple advanced degrees, remain well read after their formal education ends, and stay current with historical research, archival theory, and current events. Unlike private collectors, more women now become archivists than men, although men still dominate the highest offices in government archives.

Why Do People Collect?

According to Belk, individual collectors typically explain/justify what drives them in one or more of four ways. They

1) blame it on human nature;
2) explain a rational economic investment motive;
3) apply the medical terminology of disease such as "mania" or "addiction"; and
4) portray themselves as saviors of "lost, neglected, or endangered objects."[16]

Archivists see their work as related to number 4 and they have a fully-developed theoretical basis for their profession and its perspective.

Rendell observed that while many collectors explain their interest as intellectual, they reveal a highly emotional component as well. Muensterberger claims the urge to collect manifests itself as "an unrelenting need, even hunger, for acquisitions." If the urge to collect contains emotional components manifesting themselves in many ways, what are those ways?

Connection to history

The connection to history appears frequently. Rendell acclaims the world of historical letters and documents as "a virtual time machine that takes us into the lives of those persons in culture and history whose genius has touched us, whose lives and accomplishments have inspired us, whose efforts have created our heritage and influenced our present.... Letters and documents are the most direct link we can have to the heroes and heroines, villains, and ordinary people of the past."[17] Having historical documents nearby provides inspiration or reflection or comfort. Rendell describes one collector who, when her life became difficult, reflected on the lives of those who created documents she owned and how they got through difficult times. Dr. A. S. W. Rosenbach, one of the curators who helped develop the collections at the Huntington Library, among other collections, wrote, "Although the printed books relating to America are fascinating, autographs make the incidents they describe alive and vivid to us. Every true collector is greatly moved when he sees the autograph of a great personage in his country's history.... The printed word must have a certain coldness and formality.... But words written down by the actor himself as he helps to complete the drama are personal things which unfailingly appeal to the imagination."[18] Malcolm Forbes wrote in his memoir "Unquestionably my favorite among the [many different] collections are the autograph...documents.... Such documents...remind us that these are more than historical figures—they are people pouring their hopes, sadness, reactions, and directions onto paper. Their letters make flesh and blood of key figures in our country's history.... Somehow, when you put your hands on the things and see the words as they were penned, it brings to stark history a human dimension that makes the dead alive."[19]

Clearly these people aren't talking about a program designed to capture evidence of governmental activity. While archivists must capture evidence, they also share some of the emotional response described above. The higher the emotional response, the greater the "trophy" quality the document has. Belk explains it this way: "The ways in which as feeling individuals we desire materials which come to us from a [distant time] plays a large part in structuring our relationship to these distances."[20] As he notes, "The material nature of objects means that they, and they alone, have the capacity to carry the past physically into the present." (Belk, 170) Regardless of what has befallen it between the moment of creation and the present, the document or object retains the historical reality with which it came into being. In large part that historical content and connection gives them "their glow of desirability." (Belk, 172) This glow of desirability very much comes into play and transforms a bit of historical evidence into a revered icon, like the founding documents at all levels of government and the private papers or possessions of important people.

Prestige and Competition

Belk speculates that collectors gain a feeling of mastery, competence, or success based on the quality and quantity of their possessions and that, in a materialistic society, their collections broadly provide an index to their successfulness in life in general. (Belk, 87) Like the non-verbal language of clothing and cars, Belk asserts that collections can say things about collectors that they would find socially unacceptable to express aloud. (Belk, 90)

Adding to their perceived status as the owners of something rare and valuable, collectors have a good chance of becoming real experts within their narrow range of collecting. They may display their expertise through the discrimination exhibited in their selections.[21] Even those who do not share an enthusiasm for collecting may admire the dedication, passion, and discriminative abilities exhibited by the collection, especially when it includes rare, highly valued, and unique items. (Belk, 88) In keeping with the emotional basis for collecting, collectors "privilege the authentic, and the genuine or real over its opposites." (Belk, 286) Belk argues that collectors value rare objects because rarity provides both more challenge and a greater feeling of accomplishment after a successful foray. It also confers higher status within the circle of collectors of similar objects. (Belk, 74)

Collectors acquire things in many ways, and frequently the process of acquiring a document adds to the emotional value of the collection. Some collectors develop a weekly routine centered on searching for additions to their collections. Belk observed that collectors look at shopping as a treasure hunt, an adventure, a quest, a form of entertainment. (Belk, 72) He also noted that collectors frequently refer to "hunting for material to add to the collection" as an analogy that promotes an image of "cunning, stealth, patience, prowess, competition and ultimate success with the acquisition" (Belk, 183–184) Thus, Belk argues, the challenge and mastery implicit in the hunt metaphor relate to the collectors' feelings of accomplishment and success. (Belk, 93)

Collecting high-value material can become a highly competitive activity. Like athletes, collectors may seek out others sharing a common passion to learn from them or to compare their collections. The collector can also compete against a self-imposed standard of excellence. Collecting takes place within a narrower arena than general consuming, and this narrowing enhances the competitive fervor. Shopping and competition combine most visibly at public auctions. (Belk, 68)

Sense of Community

Document collectors have a number of organizations they can join. Private collectors join the Manuscript Society, the Professional Autograph Dealers Association, and the Universal Autograph Collectors Club. Archivists join Society of American Archivists, Council of State Archivists, National Association of Government Archives and Records Administrators, and any number of regional and local organizations. In their respective organizational meetings, individual collectors and institutional collectors can talk about the issues they face, giving and receiving advice and validation in the course of the conversation. Over time they develop a genuine community of friends they can easily define. However, such feelings of community do not lessen the rivalry among those same collectors. (Belk, 93–94)

Control

"A number of researchers have suggested that the motivation to be in control underlies possessive behaviour."[22] Since people can easily control objects, they can accumulate them by keeping them for themselves or making simple transfers as gifts, sales, and bequests.[23] People "can control their collections as they can few other matters in this world...and the ground for this control rests in our ability to select or discard items for inclusion in our collections, and then to manipulate those which we choose as we wish." (Belk, 178) After all, the collector alone decides everything about the collection; he "is king of all he surveys." (Belk, 196)

Why Do Non-governmental Institutions Collect?

Some of the same psychological factors involved in individual collecting appear in institutional collecting. Institutions become the extended self of the supporting society. Communities large and small support cultural heritage institutions, including archives, as a way to preserve and highlight their cultural heritage and provide what Pearce calls a cultural narrative that reveals/explains their respective culture and how it came to be. According to Pearce, "The power of [any] cultural narrative...rests less on its 'historical reality' than in its standing as 'communal fiction'.... The communal fallacy is powerful enough to create the extended meaning of historical depth which we can see, and of which the collecting process is a part."[24] Collections of either documents or artifacts "narrate world-views of knowledge and moral understanding in relation to the individual hero or heroine, family and society, the past and exotic." (Pearce, 412) Frequently these world-view reflect prove "a social construct in which apparent sense is created from the range of possibilities and discontinuities." (Pearce, 412)

The founders of early American repositories understood the part they played in creating the new republic's cultural narrative. The early collectors and keepers all focused on their collections' use to historians. As the previous chapters have demonstrated, in the absence of governmental repositories for historical documents, private historical societies grew up to fill the need as collectors tried to anticipate what historians and biographers would need.

Why Do Governments Collect?

By the nineteenth century, Europe and America had an established, if somewhat different, a "panoramic view into which all aspects of human history and human relationships are fitted" (Pearce, 132) into the natural world. Beginning with the British Museum in 1753, the great national and civic museums that grew up in the eighteenth and nineteenth centuries expressed some aspect of that view, and received support and validation from the economic prosperity of the cultures that created them. They brought visitors "a new view of the historical past and of the material which had come down from it." (Pearce, 134) They further inspired an application of scientific principles to archeological exploration of the past. Out of that grew the discipline of "scientific history" to counteract the artificial creation of cultural narratives. As chapter 3 shows, in the United States, the historians drove the movement to create government archives. They wanted governments to retain their archives so they, the historians, could have access to the raw materials they needed.

By the late twentieth century, the rationale for government collections does not give priority to serving historians. I explore the modern rationale of archives much more deeply in chapter 6, so will simply summarize here the general rationale currently understood as the reason for government archives:

1) Records protect life by documenting the infrastructure of communities, thus making it possible to maintain health delivery systems for water and sewage and to create escape routes in cases of emergency.

2) Records protect property ownership through land records, probate records, divorce settlements.

3) Records establish order and document the operation of government. The records of government demonstrate the acts and effectiveness of democracy.

4) Records underpin our nation's information infrastructure;

5) Records protect tranquility by validating personal and group histories.[25]

Modern archival theory suggests that if archivists document the issues laid out above, historians will have what they need.

How Do Collectors Let Go?

Individual collectors acquire and relinquish collections according to personal interests. Sanford Mock explains the whole cycle quite gracefully. Mock spent his career as a Los Angeles stockbroker and started collecting as he approached retirement.

"From 1980–1997 I collected antique documents of various kinds, primarily with a financial orientation. I started with beautifully designed and engraved stocks and bonds, mostly 19th century.

"Then to non-beautiful, plain black and white Confederate war bonds, printed on thin, flimsy paper, which turned out to be surprisingly durable. Next I began acquiring stock and bond certificates signed by famous persons, notably the robber barons of the late 19th century.

"Then back a century or more to the American colonial period. Simultaneously with that quest, I began accumulating signed documents of our Presidents....

"After I had acquired two or three items signed by every American President, I went the other way. That is, I stopped acquiring and began distributing. The concept of sharing had a lot of appeal. I either gave away or sold almost all the valuable pieces.... Parting with all this material was painful at first. But I learned that the main pleasure is in the acquisition rather than the contemplation. So the trauma dissipated soon."[26]

Belk's study confirms that Mock had a normal reaction to parting with a collection. Belk reports that "attention to a collection is matched...by suffering caused by its loss."[27] He goes on to report that "the collector usually gives considerable thought to the destination of the collection, particularly as he himself starts to grow older."[28] As I indicate in chapter 1, many institutions have benefit from this concern.

Comparing Individual Collectors, Governmental Archivists, and Institutional Collectors

Individual Collectors	Government Archivists	Non-governmental Institutional Curators
Collect in some specific areas and not in others	Collect in some specific areas and not in others	Collect in some specific areas and not in others
Decide for themselves what items to collect	Decisions to acquire or not may involve a more highly systematized process	Decisions to acquire or not may involve a more highly systematized process
Have their own resources to support their decisions	Have the power of the state funding and supporting them	Have the power of the institution funding and supporting them
Own the materials they acquire and care for	Do not own the materials they acquire and care for	Do not own the materials they acquire and care for
Do not have to justify what they collect or why	Must justify what they collect and why	Must justify what they collect and why
Acquire what suits them	Are implicitly and explicitly bound to acquire materials for the benefit of others	Are implicitly and explicitly bound to acquire materials for the benefit of others
Can justify collecting as a playful, fun activity	Demonstrate the seriousness of the work by documenting appraisal and acquisitions policies and process carried out by the government	Demonstrate the seriousness of the work by documenting appraisal and acquisitions policies and process carried out by the institution
May collect on the basis of a financial investment criterion	May collect on the basis of a public relations investment criterion	May collect on the basis of a public relations investment criterion
Look at the collection in any way they want	Look at the collection through an intellectualized justification for having it	Look at the collection through an intellectualized justification for having it

Unlike private collectors, government archives and other institutions rarely let go of collections. As government archives moved into new buildings, "the vacuum of the building's hollow interior sucked in records,"[29] which, in hindsight and with the benefit of more sophisticated appraisal theories and techniques, it should not have. Decades later, archivists find useless collections very hard to let go of for a variety of reasons having to do with bureaucratic complexity, institutional politics, and human nature. Even when everyone agrees that the historic value of a particular series of papers probably doesn't justify the space it occupies, the process of undoing everything that has gone into arranging, describing, and preserving it seems daunting and painful, as well as wasteful.[30]

Where Do Historical Documents on the Market Come From?

Much material comes from the descendants of creators or recipients of historic documents. They part with them at the point when they understand that the market value exceeds sentimental value. Collectors, both private individuals and institutions, in the process of selling off collections provide another source.[31] Unfortunately theft from government offices and repositories also adds to the available inventory.

Dealers

Dealers stay in business by pleasing everyone—private collectors, institutional curators, and government archivists alike. For the sake of their business they must understand the perspective of their clients, and many go to extraordinary lengths to maintain good relationships with clients.[32] So, when approached by an archivist in search of a document newly discovered to have disappeared, dealers must instantly assess a wide variety of factors as they decide how to respond. Many cooperate when they see no jeopardy in it but will not if they see a threat to a valued client relationship. Some manage to navigate the choppy waters of cooperating with an archivist and retaining a cordial relationship with a client holding a public record that the archivist wants. But as a general rule, dealers, especially dealers with high-end clients, "never divulge information about clients."[33]

Notes

1. Werner Muensterberger, *Collecting: An Unruly Passion* (Princeton: Princeton University Press, 1994), 3.

2. Edmund Berkeley, Jr., Herbert E. Klingelhofer, and Kenneth Rendell eds., *Autographs and Manuscripts: A Collector's Manual* (New York: Charles Scribner's Sons, 1978); Mary A. Benjamin, *Autographs: A Key to Collecting* (New York: Bowker, 1946); David Lowenthal, *The Past is a Foreign Country* (Cambridge: Cambridge University Press, 1985); David Lowenthal, *The Heritage Crusade and the Spoils of History* (Cambridge: Cambridge University Press, 1998); Werner Muensterberger, *Collecting: An Unruly Passion* (Princeton: Princeton University Press, 1994); Russell W. Belk, *Collecting in a Consumer Society* (New York: Routledge, 1995); Susan M. Pearce, *On Collecting: An Investigation into Collecting in the European Tradition* (London: Routledge, 1995), 3.

3. Pearce, *On Collecting*, 3.

4. Pearce, *On Collecting*, 22.

5. Muensterberger, *Collecting*, 4.

6. Pearce, *On Collecting*, 23.

7. Belk, *Collecting in a Consumer Society*, 235.

8. Muensterberger, *Collecting*, 6.

9. Kevin M. Gutherie, *New York Historical Society: Lessons from One Nonprofit's Long Struggle for Survival* (San Francisco: Jossey-Bass, 1996).

10. Pearce, *On Collecting*, 367–369.

11. Muensterberger, *Collecting*, 8.

12. Kenneth Rendell, *History Comes to Life: Collecting Historical Letters and Documents* (Norman: University of Oklahoma Press, 1995), 6.

13. Rendell, *History Comes to Life*, 6.

14. Rendell, *History Comes to Life*, 6–7.

15. Belk, *Collecting in a Consumer Society*, 99.

16. Belk, *Collecting in a Consumer Society*, 78–81.

17. Rendell, *History Comes to Life*, 1–2.

18. Abraham S. Wolf Rosenbach, *Books and Bidders* (Boston: Little, Brown, 1927), 284.

19. Malcolm Forbes, *More Than I Have Dreamed: A Lifetime of Collecting* (New York: Simon & Schuster, 1989), 210–212.

20. Belk, *Collecting in a Consumer Society*, 245.

21. Belk, *Collecting in a Consumer Society*, 354.

22. Pearce, *On Collecting*, 174.

23. Belk, *Collecting in a Consumer Society*, 170.

24. Pearce, *On Collecting*, 406.

25. Council of State Archivists, *The State of State Records: A Status Report on State Archives and Records Management Programs in the United States* (Iowa City, Iowa: Council of State Archivists, 2007), 11–13, http://www.statearchivists.org/reports/2007ARMreport (April 15, 2011).

26. Sanford J. Mock, *Document Stories: A Pastiche of Stories* (Los Angeles: Elton-Wolf, 2002), vii–viii.

27. Belk, *Collecting in a Consumer Society*, 175.

28. Belk, *Collecting in a Consumer Society*, 248.

29. Leonard Rapport, "No Grandfather Clause: Reappraising Accessioned Records," *American Archivist* 44 (Spring 1981): 143–144.

30. Rapport, "No Grandfather Clause," 143–150.

31. Government archives destroy unwanted materials rather than sell them.
32. John M. Taylor, *History in Your Hand* (Westport, CT: Praeger, 1997), 4.
33. Rendell, *History Comes to Life*, 7.

Chapter 5

Replevin

In October 1975, the case *of North Carolina vs. B.C. West, Jr.,* went to trial in Pasquotank, North Carolina, without a jury. West, a manuscripts and autographs dealer, had offered two colonial era North Carolina county court documents for sale, and the Archivist of North Carolina initiated a replevin action against him. The court found that while the law was with the state, the age of the documents and their indefinite length of time out of archival custody warranted an equity ruling for West.

The state appealed to the North Carolina Court of Appeals and the case went to trial in August 1976. The Court of Appeals reversed the previous ruling, holding that a public record cannot be destroyed, defaced, or given up without the authority of a legislative body.[1] In other words, mere possession does not constitute ownership. "The court cited *City of New York* v. *Lent,* 51 Barb. 19 (1868), which held that there can be no bona fide purchase of a public document until a duly authorized public authority has legally disposed of the document."[2]

West appealed to the North Carolina Supreme Court. On June 13, 1977, the Supreme Court upheld the Court of Appeals ruling.[3] The majority opinion "found that sovereignty does not lapse—that at some time between the outbreak of the Revolution and the Treaty of Paris in 1783 the sovereignty of the crown became the sovereignty of the state. Thus public ownership of the [documents] had never been broken." Further, the judge observed, "These documents, being bills of indictment, bear upon their face notice to all the world that they were part of the court records of the Colony of North Carolina and, therefore, the property of the State." He found that "a public record created by and for the state can be legally disposed of only by the state, and there is no evidence that the...documents had ever been so disposed." The court declared that it had no authority to reimburse the defendant; "only the legislature could authorize state funds for such a purpose." West relinquished the documents in November 1977.[4]

What's Replevin?

North Carolina had brought a replevin action against West. A replevin action occurs when the plaintiff claims that the accused unjustly holds something that belongs to the plaintiff, and the plaintiff wants it back. The accused may have come to hold it in many different ways. Perhaps the plaintiff loaned it to the accused for a set period of time, and that time has gone by. Perhaps the plaintiff lost it, and the accused found it and will not return it. Perhaps someone stole it and gave it or sold it to the accused. Replevin does not imply guilt of any wrong-doing beyond holding property that the plaintiff wants back.

The use of replevin in English law goes back to at least the middle of the thirteenth century. Today, replevin laws exist all over the world as civil, not criminal, actions. A replevin action grows out of the plaintiff's inability to recover his or her property without help, so he or she turns to the justice system for help with recovery of the actual property, not its monetary value.

To initiate a replevin action, the plaintiff must file a claim with the court. While state laws differ in detail, all expect the plaintiff to show

1) that the plaintiff owns the property or a has legal right to possession of it.

2) that the accused has no right to hold the property.

3) that the property did not leave the plaintiff's possession as a result of any adverse legal action.

4) the approximate value of the property.[5]

If, in the course of a replevin action, the parties learn that the property in question no longer exists (and was not willfully destroyed), the action ceases.

Replevin actions occur in regard to a wide variety of materials, but here we will focus on replevin as it applies to historical documents. Interest in replevin has increased among documents collectors and dealers in the last decade or two, largely because the ability to sell historical documents has increased dramatically. Before Internet auctions, most non-collectors could not assess the value of documents in their possession, nor did they know a dealer in historical documents. Indeed, they might not have realized that historical documents have an active and lucrative market. Today, television shows like *Antiques Road Show* introduce the public to that market on a weekly basis. As a result, people have become aware that those old documents that have passed down through the family may have substantial monetary value. They may not have any clear idea as to how the family acquired them and whether or not the law allows them to hold them, but they know they can sell them online.

What's a Public Document?

The definition of a public document varies depending on the context of the use of the term. In some contexts, we use the term "public" to imply "not confidential." In others we use the term "public" to mean a document created by a public body in the line of duty. The second definition claims our attention here.

The states define what they regard as public documents in a variety of ways that tend to follow several common themes. I have added the emphasis in the passages below.

1) Some definitions link public documents to the act of creation or reception. For example, Maine uses the term "record" to refer to a public document and defines them as "all documentary material, regardless of media or characteristics, *made or received and maintained by an agency in accordance with law or rule or in the transaction of its official business*." Maine law makes clear that the definition does not include the extra copies of printed or processed material that have been retained, but it does apply to local as well as state documents.[6] Maine's Secretary of State website offers examples: "Ledgers recording the official business of cities, towns, or plantations, such as minutes of meetings, charters or records of organization, ordinances, etc. Documents recorded by municipal clerks and retained by them. Records of government institutions: poor farms, jails, public hospitals, reform schools, public schools."[7]

2) Other states link the expenditure of public money to the definition of public documents. Georgia, for instance, asserts that a document "*created or received in the performance of a public duty or paid for by public funds* by a governing body are deemed to be public property and shall constitute a record of public acts," including local government officials.[8]

3) Some states make clear that records take forms other than paper. California defines public documents as including "any writing containing information relating to the conduct of the public's business prepared, owned, used, or retained by a state or local agency *regardless of physical form or characteristics*."[9]

4) New Jersey tries to cover all aspects described above by defining a public record as "any paper, written or printed book, document or drawing, map or plan, photograph, microfilm, sound-recording or similar device, or any copy thereof which has been made or is required by law to be received for filing, indexing, or reproducing by any officer, commission, agency or authority of the State or of any political subdivision thereof, including subordinate boards thereof, or that has been received by any such officer, commission, agency or authority of the State or of any political subdivision thereof, including subordinate boards thereof, in connection with the transaction of public business."[10]

Some states include in their official publications a rationale for the importance of government control of public documents. The website for the Texas State Library and Archives Commission explains that "the disappearance of government records into private hands deprives the public of access to important historical information that helps us understand the history of our state and nation. Government records document government actions for the review of the citizens. The inappropriate transfer of such records into private hands greatly restricts access to them which in turn hampers government accountability."[11]

Virginia explains it like this: "Public records contain a wealth of invaluable information related to governmental actions that may be of concern to citizens of the commonwealth. The removal of these documents from public access hinders the ability of the general public to understand the consequences of actions by government agencies. This disrupts a key element of government accountability and unfairly takes useful historical resources out of the public's reach."[12]

The Texas State Library and Archives Commission (TSLAC) website explains why they care about these issues by explaining that "Texas has lost hundreds of official historical government records, from its public archives particularly from the Colonial, Republic, and early Statehood periods, and many have ended up in private collections.... TSLAC is deeply concerned about the number of official state and local government records, many that once resided in the Texas State Archives that have begun to appear for sale in auction catalogs and on eBay and other commercial web sites."[13]

Regardless of whether public documents go to an archives or a recycle center, state laws and retention schedules put government officials in charge of their disposal. Alabama gives the responsibility to its state records commission. *"The [Alabama] State Records Commission shall be charged with the responsibility of determining which state records shall be permanently preserved because of historical value, which state records may be destroyed or otherwise disposed of after they have been microfilmed and which state records may be destroyed or otherwise disposed of without microfilming."*[14]

In Georgia, "state law requires that the destruction of records shall occur only through the operation of an approved retention schedule. The disposition of records that have been discarded legally will be well documented and easily identified from the retention schedule."[15]

In Texas, "it is illegal for government records to be sold or alienated from public custody unless done in accordance with established, legal retention procedures."[16]

Many laws forbid the private ownership of public records. In Georgia, "the destruction of records shall occur only through the operation of an approved retention schedule. *The records shall not be placed in the custody of private individuals or institutions or semi-private organizations unless authorized by retention schedules*."[17]

Maine amended its recovery of public records law in 2003 to clarify that "a person may not sell or transfer a [public] record unless specifically authorized by law." Additionally, upon notice, records believed to be government records may not be sold or given away until a final determination of their status is made.[18]

Tennessee sees public records as public property, which "must remain forever in public custody, and *at no time can public records legally be owned, traded, sold, or bought by members of the general public.... The private sale of these records is strictly prohibited* according to the so-called replevin law."[19]

"New Jersey public records cannot be legally held by another party without a depository agreement duly executed by, or with the approval of, the New Jersey Division of Archives and Records Management."[20]

Some laws authorize certain government officials to attempt to recover alienated documents, i.e., documents that should be in an archives but are not. The Virginia Public Records Act, for instance, forbids the separation of any public record from public ownership and "*gives the Librarian of Virginia, the State Archivist, or any public official charged with the care of these documents the ability to petition the appropriate judicial authority for its return.*"[21]

Some state laws apply current standards back through time. Maine holds that unless the evidence clearly indicates otherwise, records that were once in the custody of the state or a local government were not *lawfully* alienated from that custody.[22]

New Jersey declares that all laws about public records were "retrospective, retroactive and founded in common law and colonial and early state statutes regarding the preservation of public records. Through the New Jersey State Constitution of 2 July 1776, which adopted the full extent of colonial law then in place, and subsequent constitutions and legislation, [the New Jersey Statutes on replevin] is applicable and enforceable with respect to official records of both the Colony and State of New Jersey and its subdivisions."[23]

Some states detail specifically how the laws against private possession of public documents should be executed. California law directs that "whenever the Secretary [of State], in consultation with the archivist, has reasonable grounds to believe that a record belonging to the state or a local agency is in the possession of a person, organization, or institution not authorized by law to possess those records, the secretary may issue a written notice demanding that person, organization, or institution to do either of the following within 20 calendar days of receiving the notice."[24]

If the person, organization, or institution returns the California document, "the secretary or a local agency that receives the record shall issue to that person, organization, or institution a copy or digital image of the record, which shall be certified as a true copy of the record that was returned to the state or local agency, and dated on the same day the record was returned."[25]

New Mexico law says that if "a particular public record is not in the hands of the official custodian...[but] in the possession of a private party or parties," the public officer "shall initiate an act of replevin."[26] If the holder of the document returns it, the New Mexico may "duplicate the document and...give the private party a copy and keep the original public record."[27]

Only California law protects institutional holders of public documents by recognizing "an organization or institution having physical custody of a record shall be exempt...if the organization or institution meets" two requirements. First, it must "follow professional practices recommended by the Society of American Archivists...for the management, care, and preservation of historical records." Second, "all records it receives or maintains are subject to inspection to the same extent that the records would be subject to inspection...if received or maintained by a public agency."[28]

All states encourage the voluntary return of public documents. For instance, the "New Jersey State Archives invites the voluntary return of any such documents to the State of New Jersey. In such instances, the State Archives will suspend formal demand and legal process to recover such documents and will, upon receipt of them, acknowledge the same as a donation to the State Archives. The State may also exercise discretion in negotiating mutually beneficial terms for the return of such documents and formal acknowledgment of their legal ownership. This may include planned public and/or media events."[29]

State laws vary greatly, and they determine the parameters an archivist has for acting on or negotiating in a replevin action. If the state has the authority and resources, archivists will act to retrieve alienated documents. However, the actual pursuit and prosecution must happen through the state's Attorney General's (AG) office.

A Council of State Archivists (CoSA) report notes that "while most state archives and records management programs have sufficient authority in law or regulation to establish policies and procedures for current records and to ensure that those of long-term significance are preserved, most do not have commensurate resources, enforcement mechanisms, or mandates to assert this authority effectively."[30] Since they must go through their AG's office, convincing their own enforcement arm to act may present the first hurdle they must cross. Regardless of their real circumstances, on paper and in practice most states work with a variety of options.

Some state laws require that the archivist retrieve the original; the archivist has no option but to do that. Others do not have that requirement built into their laws. In those states, the archivist can decide whether to pursue the original or accept a copy to place in the historical record. As you might imagine, the archivist's decision will depend on 1) whether the AG's office shows an interest in the case, and 2) the monetary and symbolic value of the document.

Archivists understand that reclaiming documents causes a lot of pain to the holder, and they have devised a variety of ways to soften the blow. Because states do not want to pay for something they claim they already own, they may seek to compensate the holder of the materials without outwardly buying the document. Some seek out a cultural organization to buy the document that will then turn around and donate the document to the archives. The state may pay a "caretaker's fee" to help cover the expense of caring for the document over time. If the holder paid for conservation or restoration work, the state may agree to cover part of that cost. Archivists will also arrange for an independent appraisal of the document and provide the holder with a document that shows that the holder donated the document to the state, thus making it possible for the donor to claim a charitable tax deduction.[31]

Outside the reward of money, many states make a point of holding highly publicized "coming home" parties for the documents. They set up a display so visitors can see the documents, officials make speeches, and everyone enjoys the refreshments. For maximum exposure, archivists invite the press.

What about Copies?

In states with weak replevin laws or in cases that do not interest the AG's office, the archivist may negotiate for a copy of the document. Archivists have long dealt with copies. Since 1975, federal law has allowed copies of documents to serve as evidence, provided no question can arise about the authenticity of the copy.[32] So, while historians and attorneys regard the original as preferable, originals are really needed only for symbolic purposes. I cover the issue of copies much more deeply in chapter 6.

How Do Others Handle the Problem of Public Documents in Private Hands?

The British have two responses to the private ownership of public documents. Under UK law, "certain cultural objects more than 50 years of age and valued above specified financial thresholds will require an individual licence for export out of the United Kingdom whether on a permanent or temporary basis."[33] That includes historical documents. The Export and Loans Unit within the Museums, Libraries, and Archives Council (MLA) in the Department of Culture, Media, and Sport controls the export of historical documents. It has established a clearly defined protocol in its *UK Export Licensing for Cultural Goods: Procedures for Exporters of Works of Art and Other Cultural Goods*.[34] In essence, the exporter must get a license by applying to the Export and Loans Unit. That body will turn the request over to an Expert Advisor to consider whether the document in question has "outstanding national importance" while striking a balance between "the protection of the national heritage; the rights of the owner selling the goods; the exporter or overseas purchaser; and the position and reputation of the UK as an international art market." (p. 3) In the case of manuscripts, the Expert Advisor "may recommend that the UK national interest may be satisfied by the retention of a copy, and that the originals should be granted an export licence" provided they do not infringe on the rights of the copyright holder. (p. 5) The Expert Advisor looks to a set of criteria known as the Waverley Criteria for guidance. He or she look at an item as it relates to UK history, asking, "Is it so closely connected with our history and national life that its departure would be a misfortune?" They also consider its aesthetics, asking, "Is it of outstanding aesthetic importance?" Finally they consider scholarship, asking, "Is it of outstanding significance for the study of some particular branch of art, learning or history?"(pp. 9–11) If the MLA determines that a document may not leave the country, it then must find a purchaser within the country to acquire the materials; the MLA does not simply deny the would-be seller the sale.[35] While the MLA regulations apply to all UK members, Scotland holds "certain public records" as *extra commercium*.[36] The legal phrase *res extra commercium* defines a concept that goes back to at least Roman law to mean that once something has been dedicated to public use, it cannot be alienated unless the governing body legally disavows its claim. The phrase itself does not appear in American law and court actions, but Oliver Metzger argues that the concept does—as in the North Carolina vs. B.C. West case—and the American legal system should adopt the phrase rather than hint at it.[37]

The export licence process applies to both personal and public papers headed out of the country. British archivists view the sale of public papers within the United Kingdom the way archivists in the United States do: public records selected for permanent preservation, as defined by the Public Record Act of 1958, may not be sold "on the open market" and may be held only by designated custodians.[38]

Notes

1. 31 N.C. App. 431; William S. Price, "N.C. v. B. C. West, Jr.," *American Archivist* 41 (January 1978): 22.

2. Price, "N.C. v. B.C. West, Jr.," 23.

3. 293 N.C. 18; Price, "N.C. v. B.C. West, Jr.," 22.

4. Price, "N.C. v. B. C. West, Jr.," 22–24.

5. Menzi L. Behrnd-Klodt, *Navigating Legal Issues in Archives* (Chicago: Society of American Archivists, 2008), 169. Behrnd-Koldt summarizes the legal history and procedures related to replevin as it relates to public documents.

6. Maine Revised Statutes Title 5: Administrative Procedures and Services: Part 1: State Departments: Chapter 6: State Archivist Heading: Pl 1973, C. 625, §16 (New) §92-A. Definitions, http://www.mainelegislature.org/legis/statutes/5/title5sec92-A.html (Nov. 9, 2009).

7. "Involved in the Purchase or Sale of Government Records? It's Illegal! Please Consider the Following," http://www.maine.gov/sos/arc/replvnot.htm (Oct. 25, 2009).

8. Georgia State and Court Records (O.C.G.A. 50-18-102) and Local Government Records (O.C.G.A. 50-18-99), http://sos.georgia.gov/archives/how_may_we_help_you/policy_statement/default.htm (Oct. 14, 2009).

9. California Government Code, Title I Division 7 Chapter 3.01 Section 6204 (a) (2), http://www.leginfo.ca.gov/pub/09-10/bill/asm/ab_1201-1250/ab_1245_bill_20091011_chaptered.html (April 16, 2011).

10. New Jersey Statutes, 47:3–16, http://www.njarchives.org/links/pdf/pl1953c410.pdf (April 17, 2011).

11. Texas State Library and Archives Commission, "Sale of Government Records," http://www.tsl.state.tx.us/arc/sale.html (April 17, 2011).

12. Library of Virginia, "The Sale of Government Records Is Illegal!," http://www.lva.virginia.gov/public/replevin.htm (April 17, 2011).

13. Texas State Library and Archives Commission, "Sale of Government Records," http://www.tsl.state.tx.us/arc/sale.html (April 17, 2011).

14. Code of Alabama, Section 41-13-21, http://alisondb.legislature.state.al.us/acas/CodeOfAlabama/1975/41-13-21.htm (April 17, 2011).

15. Georgia O.C.G.A. 50-18-102(b), http://sos.georgia.gov/archives/how_may_we_help_you/policy_statement/default.htm (14 Oct. 2009).

16. Texas State Library and Archives Commission, "Sale of Government Records," http://www.tsl.state.tx.us/arc/sale.html (April 17, 2011).

17. Georgia, O.C.G.A. 50-18-102.

18. Maine 5 MRSA 95-A, Protection and Recovery of Public Records.

19. Tennessee State Library and Archives, http://tennessee.gov/tsla/aps/replevin.htm (Oct. 25, 2009).

20. New Jersey Department of State, Public Records and Archives, *New Jersey Missing or Alienated Records of the State of New Jersey Public Notice*, http://www.nj.gov/state/darm/links/missingdocuments.html (Sept. 10, 2011).

21. Virginia, "The Sale of Government Records."

22. Maine Revised Statutes, Title 5: Administrative Procedures and Services Part 1: State Departments Chapter 6: State Archivist Heading: Pl 1973, C. 625, §16 (New), http://www.mainelegislature.org/legis/statutes/5/title5sec95-A.html (Oct. 25, 2009).

23. New Jersey, *Missing or Alienated Records.*

24. California, Section 1, Chapter 3.01 (commencing with Section 6204) is added to Division 7 of Title 1 of the Government Code California, Official California Legislative Information, http://www.leginfo.ca.gov/pub/09-10/bill/asm/ab_1201-1250/ab_1245_bill_20091011_chaptered.html (Jan. 4, 2010).

25. California, Section 1, Chapter 3.01.

26. New Mexico, 14-5-1 to 14-5-10 NMSA 1978, "Public Records Recovery Act," http://www.nmcpr.state.nm.us/info/14-5NMSA.pdf (Oct. 29, 2009).

27. New Mexico, Recovery Act.

28. California, Section 1, Chapter 3.01.

29. New Jersey, *Missing or Alienated Records.*

30. Council of State Archivists, *Report of the Blue Ribbon Panel: A Supplement to* The State of State Records*: A Status Report on State Archives and Records Management Programs in the United States* (Iowa City: Council of State Archivists, 2007), 5, http://www.statearchivists.org/reports/2007-ARMreport/BRPreport-final.pdf (April 15, 2011).

31. The author has gleaned these strategies from various private conversations with various state archivists over the course of writing this book.

32. Gary M. Peterson and Trudy Huskamp Peterson, *Archives and Manuscripts: Law* (Chicago: Society of American Archivists, 1985), 89, http://www2.archivists.org/sites/all/files/Archives&Mss-Law.pdf (10 Sept. 2011).

33. Museums, Libraries, and Archives Council, "Exporting Licensing," http://www.mla.gov.uk/what/cultural/export (May 13, 2011).

34. Museums, Libraries, and Archives Council, *UK Export Licensing for Cultural Goods: Procedures for Exporters of Works of Art and Other Cultural Goods, a Museums,*

Libraries, and Archives Council Notice (London: MLA, 2010), www.mla.gov.uk/what/cultural/export/~/media/Files/pdf/2010/AELU/UK_Export_Licensing_guidance_for_exporters_of_works_of_art_and_other_cultural_goods.ashx (May 13, 2011).

35. For an example of the process, see Department of Culture, Media, and Sport, "Case 2: The Papers of James Bruce, 8th Earl of Elgin," *Report of the Reviewing Committee on the Export of Works of Art and Objects of Cultural Interest, 2008–2009* (London: MLA, 2009), 29, http://www.mla.gov.uk/~/media/Files/pdf/2009/RCEWA_Annual_report_08-09_sm_2 (May 13, 2011).

36. Museums, Libraries, and Archives Council, *UK Export Licensing for Cultural Goods*, 6.

37. Oliver Metzger, Making the Doctrine of *res extra commercium* Visible in United States Law, *Texas Law Review* 74 (1996): 615.

38. Email to the author from James Travers, head of the Manuscript Sales Monitoring Service of the National Archives (UK) (May 12, 2011).

Chapter 6

Perspectives

"It is not at all remarkable that honorable men should honestly differ on [the ownership of public archives], just as they differ on politics, religion, fishing lures, or the merits of modern art."[1]

The conflict between archivists and dealer/collectors comes down to a matter of perspective and what theory one applies to the circumstances. In this chapter, I compare the perspectives of the two sides.

Major Issues in the Debate

What's Being Argued Over?

In all cases, the dispute centers on the physical ownership of the document. Copyrights do not apply to public documents, so the right to control the intellectual content does not come into question.

Where Will the Argument Take Place?

According to Metzger, the United States has relied on the laws of the location (*lex situs*) of a moveable property to determine the status, but he sees that dominance declining. Europeans, he claims, rely more heavily on the laws of the place of origins (*lex originis*).[2] That means that currently if the state of Softline finds one of its public documents in the state of Hardline, a replevin trial would take place under the laws of Hardline, not Softline. Whereas,in Europe the laws of Softline would apply.

I do not have a law degree, nor do I intend this as a book of legal advice. However, my research for this book as revealed a number of conflicting legal theories that compete for primacy in cases of ownership of historical documents. It seems useful to outline them here.

Theories That Favor the Collector

Doctrine of Accession

Common law principles acknowledge that if one person holds and cares for an item that another person then claims, "the good faith labor" of the caretaker should not be dismissed. In 1957, the unidentified author of a note in the *Yale Law Journal* argued that "the modern trend seems to be to regard the standard for replevin as one of comparative value. Thus, possession will be denied [to the party claiming original ownership] when the value of the property has been significantly enhanced."[3] The argument went that the holder protected and preserved the document so it could grow in value. Therefore, the holder/protector should benefit from that gain. Today, that trend may have shifted, as states have won cases involving ordinary public documents that have grown in value.

Laches

Laches comes from the legal maxim that "equity aids the vigilant, not those who slumber on their rights."[4] Laches recognizes that a party in a legal dispute may forfeit evidence, witnesses, and/or a defense after the passage of time. If the defendant, a dealer/collector for instance, can show others bought and sold a document while the state did nothing and that the dealer/collector would now suffer a loss because the state did not initiate a lawsuit earlier, when it could have, then the case should be dismissed because the state had slept on its rights when it did not claim the document during those early transactions.

Theories That Favor the Archivist

Extra Commercium

As I explained in chapter 5, this common law principle harks back to Roman times when certain religious articles were declared as being outside the commercial world—items one could neither sell nor buy. Though the term is not used in the United States, assigning cultural properties *extra commercium* status happens in Europe fairly consistently. Metzger argues that, in the United States, courts acknowledge the concept without naming it as such.[5] In effect archivists use the concept when they declare that a document created in the course of public business cannot become a private, saleable document. In other words, at no point in the document's life can one legally buy or sell it.

Eminent Domain

Governments have a recognized right to seize property and use it for the public good. Ordinarily *eminent domain* applies to real estate, but in theory it could apply to historical records, if the state can show the public value in taking what the holder sees as personal property. Typically, in cases of an eminent domain seizure, the state compensates the owner of the property at a fair market rate. Collectors argue that when the state demands the return of a document, the state has exercised eminent domain but without compensation, making it theft. Archivists argue that they are not stealing someone else's property—merely reclaiming their own.

Archivists' Perspective

Archivists work with a deep sense of responsibility for the safety of and access to the people's historical records. They see their duty as both a legal responsibility and as a sacred trust. They understand that present and future generations depend on them to collect and protect the evidence that policy makers used and the records of what policy makers did to create an effective and just government and society. They no longer focus on what historians need, but they do understand that they must have evidence of government decisions and actions so historians can accurately interpret and tell the stories of government and society through time.

Archivists express that perspective when they write statements like the following:

> *"The primary task of the archivist is to establish and maintain control, both physical and intellectual, over records of enduring value."*[6]
>
> *"Archivists are responsible for preserving, protecting, and providing access to all forms of information [a service which] is vital to all professions, all peoples."*[7]
>
> *"What, then, do I profess as an archivist? Most simply put: that what we archivists do is essential to the well-being of an enlightened and democratic society.... The archival record is a bastion of a just society.... The archival record assures our rights—as individuals and collectively—to our ownership of our history. As archivists who maintain the integrity of the historical record, we guard our collective past from becoming the mere creation of 'official history.'*[8]

They argue that "governments are charged with the public's interest. Government records document government actions. Transferring such records to private hands greatly restricts access to them. This in turn hampers government accountability. Public funds pay for public record and belong to the public that created them."[9] From there, archivists go to the position that "it is illegal for government records to be sold or alienated from public custody unless done in accordance with established, legal retention procedures."[10] This argument has echoes of *res extra commercium*.

Archivists who work in states that do not have specific statutes about the legality of private ownership of public documents feel strongly a need to have such legislation. As a legal responsibility, they take very seriously the state laws that they have sworn to uphold. Several state archivists I spoke with acknowledge the disruption caused by their efforts to reclaim archival documents from people who merely fall heir to them, and the archivists want to make the experience of having the documents reclaimed as painless as possible. Even so, they know that the law is the law and they have a duty to follow it.

The work of government archivists focuses on three core areas: 1) managing governmental records, 2) preserving governmental records, and 3) supporting access to and use of governmental records. As I mentioned in chapter 3, archivists see records functioning in society in five ways:

1) Records protect life by documenting the infrastructure of communities, thus making it possible to maintain services such as health delivery systems for water and sewage and to create escape routes in cases of emergency.

2) Records protect property ownership through land records, probate records, divorce settlements, "People care about what is theirs, and records are key to proving ownership."[11]

3) Records establish order and the operation of government. They reveal how federal, state, and local governments in the United States do the will of the electorate to "protect life, property, and the rights of citizens." Further, the records of government demonstrate the effectiveness of democracy. (CoSA, v)

4) Records underpin our nation's information infrastructure.

5) Records protect tranquility by validating personal and group histories. People's sense of belonging to a time or place or group begins with records, such as birth, school, marriage, and death, records. Add to those vital records the records of governmental actions and reactions to situations that effect an individual or group, and that individual or group's sense of time, place, and community becomes firm. Further, government archives document the diverse populations—individually and collectively—whose lives the government touches. Especially important, government archives of many kinds give voice to minorities such as slaves, Native Americans, and impoverished immigrants, which the popular media and non-government records render voiceless.

To have a complete historical record, government archives must be complete. "Even when the direct documentation that links a person individually to his or her community has not survived, historical records housed in government archives can restore a sense of significance and connection to the community and its collective experience." (CoSA, 13) Therefore, "Such essential records must be securely preserved and accessible to the people in perpetuity." (CoSA, v)

In sum, government archivists manage significant cultural heritage institutions. Some government archives confine their focus to supporting the information needs of state government itself, but most see themselves as providing the public with access to government information. Most have reading rooms in which researchers must use the archives' holdings, and the statistics on who used their materials support their perspective. While a few states primarily serve the administrative needs of its government, patrons that fall into that category represent 20 percent or less of the researcher population in 39 of 49 states reporting that information.

Genealogists and a wide variety of historical researchers represent the vast majority in most of the states, while non-government legal researchers represent 20 percent or more in 11 of the 49 states reporting. (CoSA, Table 4.4, 101–102) Archivists in those states have a keen awareness of their constituency, and work hard to please it. Regardless of who makes up the body of users, the archives needs a complete historical record to fulfill patrons' requests.

In 2010, Tennessee brought the full power of the state to bear against a woman in Florida who had inherited a wedding licence issued to Davy Crockett in 1805. Circumstantial evidence suggests that the owner's uncle stole it from the county courthouse where it had been issued—he had worked there during the 1930s and '40s—but the Florida woman regarded the document as part of her family's papers and refused to hand it over to Tennessee when the state requested it. Crockett never used the licence; the bride changed her mind just before the wedding, so the document had very little actual historical value. It had huge symbolic value, however, providing proof of a legendary incident in the life of one of the state's most famous sons. To exhibit the licence in all its symbolic value, the archives needed the original—and eventually got it.[12]

Archivists work resigned to the knowledge that things "walk" out of their repositories. With vast holdings that have accumulated after decades or centuries of inadequate management, archivists understand that they do not have a complete historical record. Because many of their materials have never received adequate inventorying and description, many don't know exactly what they have or should have. Archivists also understand that their budgets do not allow them to protect their holdings adequately. They would like help from collectors and dealers in restoring the historical record. They begrudge dealers who knowingly do not report public documents when they acquire them. Dealers, who stand to make a profit on a deal, and collectors, who delight in the new documents in their collections, have no patience with that position. They argue that the archivists should get their acts together and keep their stuff safe and off the market.

Without exception, archivists feel that their "unglamorous function of government"[13] does not receive the attention and support it needs. Recall that "expenditures on archives and records programs were below one-tenth of 1 percent of total expenditures by state governments across the board, with at least 13 states allocating less than one-hundredth of 1 percent specifically to records."[14] Because government archives have limited resources, they need to pick their expensive replevin battles thoughtfully. James O'Neill laid out the questions the National Archives asks when deciding to go after a document it thinks belongs to it: 1) Will the materials be made available to the public? NARA expects that public records must be available to all on an equal basis. 2) Can the public find the records? NARA expects that public records will be described and made known. 3) Will the holder make "a reasonable number of copies at a reasonable cost" if researchers request them? NARA expects that public records will be conveniently available for public use. 4) Finally, how important is the document? The content of the document must have high "consequence and value to the historical record of our past." In sum, NARA looks at "the importance of the material, its availability, and its security" as the three basic criteria.[15] In keeping with NARA's criteria, government archivists at all levels acknowledge museums, university special collections departments, and historical societies in their role as keepers of the historical record, even if they don't like it—and many don't. Individual collectors, however, do not satisfy any of NARA's criteria.[16]

Dealers and Collectors

Richard Maass, commenting on the B.C. West case, put his finger on the core issue for private collectors.

Maass wrote: "As quoted in *Time* [magazine] U.S. Archivist Wayne Grover said, 'No one at the National Archives has any inclination or intention whatsoever of attempting to gain physical possession of those historical documents currently in the possession of such responsible institutions as the great university libraries and widely respected historical associations.' Perhaps," Maass continued, "but the policy of the Archives is not static nor is its personnel. Who can say what its policy will be in ten or twenty years from today, or what the next Archivist of the United States will set as policy? Further, lest universities and historical societies take comfort, who is to decide what is a 'great' university library or a 'respected' historical association?.... And then, of course, there are you and I—and thousands like us—who have historically preserved, restored, published or permitted to be published the historical documents which are part of our heritage. Are we to be snuffed out?"[17]

Dealers and collectors appreciate the archivists' current responsibilities and perspective on their work. But, they note that until fairly recently governments ignored, neglected, and actively discarded public documents. From their perspective, those public records that survived did so because of the care of institutional and private collectors. Further, many of the documents that governments now claim have passed from one collector to another over countless transactions. The current holder may have paid thousands of dollars to acquire one of them. Dealers and collectors resent governments' modern claims that all archival documents belong in a governmental archives and must be returned there. In their eyes it amounts to legal theft.

No collector or dealer has a problem with those materials that the government can prove were stolen from the archives, but most reject claims against those materials for which governments can show no evidence that the archives ever held them. In light of governments' poor history of caring for public documents, some dealers take the position that because the National Archives did not come into existence until 1934, it should not have the right to lay claim to materials created before then, unless it can prove that the materials actually made their way into some sort of government repository. They easily extend that logic to state archives and their founding dates.

Indeed, dealers and heirs can get really passionate about the situation. Some who do not collect documents but have inherited them feel strongly enough that they say they would destroy a document before they would turn it over to the government that ignored it for a century or more. Kenneth Rendell, a highly successful dealer in very expensive documents, recently wrote,

> "When people are told that a state is making claims...they don't contact the state and give them their documents; they either destroy them or [keep them] in their collection [unavailable to] researchers. I have been in this field as a dealer for 53 years and there are hundreds upon hundreds, probably thousands, all of cases where people inherited papers and [when] they are told that if they try to sell [them to] me they will get sued and they choose to throw them away. When I started in business, the states of Virginia and South Carolina were pursuing legitimate records of theirs that were taken by Union soldiers in the Civil War. There was no question but that these were stolen, but I don't know of any case where they were given back to the states when the possessor was told this. People said to me that they did not want to get into trouble, but they didn't know anything about their having been stolen, and they were going to throw them out. That's not the way everyone would like it to be, but it is the reaction people have."[18]

Later, he wrote, "I just told someone, today, that unless they have proof [a First Lady] gave a document to their father (he worked for her) the Nat'l Archives might claim it. Chances are no one will ever hear of those documents again."[19]

Rendell's observations have support from other sources. One archivist told me of a case where a man had purchased several eighteenth-century documents, including a 1720 oath of allegiance to King George III and a county oath of office roll from a County Clerk's office. When he wanted to sell the materials, the man contacted a dealer, who explained that the document was subject to "a recovery action." The man was furious and vowed that the documents would never go back to the state. On his death bed, he made his son swear that he would never give them back to the state.

Similarly an archivist learned of a county's the first Book of Deeds, dating from the eighteenth century and containing, among other things, records of slave manumissions. He learned of it when it came up for sale on an online auction site. A reporter and a records manager from the county government figured out who had put it up for sale, and when the archivist contacted the seller, he threatened to burn the book.

Many sophisticated collectors, if they decide to sell their documents, take them overseas where governments in the United States can't reach them.

Government Inconsistency

The manuscript world contains a small and highly networked community of collectors and dealers who know one another directly and indirectly, and they share stories. Many recount unpleasant encounters with archivists. While I have heard many such stories anecdotally, I share here three I found in print.

The Lossing Case

When historian Benson John Lossing died in Dover Plains, New York, in 1891, he left "a large collection of valuable letters and records, most of which had been removed from their repositories in Virginia by soldiers during the latter part of the civil war [*sic*]." After his death, some of the collection went on sale in Boston. "The state of Virginia claimed the documents and eventually made an arrangement with Lossing's heirs," allowing them to keep some items and return others. In 1912, nearly two decades after the state's agreement with the Lossing heirs, Virginia contacted an heir who held one letter by Lafayette and one by Washington to the House of Burgesses. The state claimed that the letter belonged to the archives of Virginia and that it no longer considered the agreement with the Lossing heirs as valid.[20]

The Library of Congress Theft

Moving archives and library materials to new facilities causes a breakdown in security and staff accountability. Because the preparation for the move and the move itself often involve a lowered level of oversight, materials can easily become misplaced, overlooked, or stolen by opportunistic temporary workers or staff members.[21] All these factors prevailed for the move of the Library of Congress in the 1890s. In 1896, 71-year-old Ainsworth R. Spofford, Librarian of Congress, had to coordinate moving approximately eight hundred tons of library materials out of its headquarters in the Capitol and into a new building and reorganize the library's services. At the same time, he had to meet political challenges to his leadership within the American Library Association. "During this chaotic period, two Library employees began stealing documents directly from Spofford's locked office. Preoccupied with other matters, Spofford was oblivious to the thefts and the two robbers went completely unnoticed."[22]

The stolen documents came out of the prized collections from historian and collector Peter Force, a collection Congress had purchased in 1867 for $100,000. The collection contained a number of scrapbooks holding military and political correspondence from the Revolutionary War period, but the library had never created an inventory of their contents. Spofford kept them in his office and made them available for use only with his approval.[23]

The two thieves, a 24-year-old clerk in charge of the Music Division and a Library of Congress employee for eight years, and a 22-year-old copyright clerk with three years of experience, broke into the office and stole letters of Benedict Arnold, John Hancock, Thomas Paine, Thomas Jefferson, John Jay, John Adams, Lafayette, and Benjamin Franklin and George Washington's 1787 diary.[24] They took their spoils to William E. and Walter R. Benjamin, book and manuscripts dealers in New York. The Benjamins questioned the thieves' story from the beginning and eventually reported them in to the Secret Service.[25] A court found them guilty and fined them $200.

Reconstruction of the ransacked collection depended on Spofford's shaky memory and the Benjamins' honesty—not an inventory.[26] The Benjamins agreed to return all materials that they had purchased from the thieves, and they agreed to allow library representatives to examine their collections. After going through the dealers' inventory, library representatives claimed materials valued at least $2,000. Both Benjamin brothers also bought back items from customers who had bought stolen documents, and returned them to the Library of Congress.

As business men, the Benjamins requested compensation for returning valuable documents that the government could not prove it owned. Despite the dealers' cooperation and material help, however, the Library of Congress never reimbursed them, claiming that Congress never appropriated enough money to cover their requests.[27]

Angry at the court and the Library of Congress, William Benjamin wrote to the Librarian of Congress in November 1898 that "my service to the Government cost me about $1,500 loss in money, time, and trouble whereas the thief McElhone got off with a $200 fine." In total Benjamin estimated that he had freely returned to the Library of Congress over $7,500 worth of colonial manuscripts since he had first reported the thieves—only to receive no monetary compensation from the government for his assistance and cooperation.[28]

Yet Another Case

Scott Petersen, a collector, dealer, and intellectual property lawyer in Chicago, remembers talking with an archivist who was trying to repossess a document. Petersen asked how many similar documents the archives had. The archivist admitted they had none, and they had no record of what had become of them. "Could they have been thrown out?" Petersen asked. "It's possible," the archivist conceded, "but it's still ours and we want it."[29]

Simple Justice

Petersen has developed a legal position that he refers to as simple justice. "It would seem simple justice...that if any entity disposes of something, it could or should not be able to reclaim it without just compensation" to the current holder.[30] He has elaborated on that basic principle with six points.

1) When items are clearly stolen or misappropriated, everyone in the archival/collector community should help repatriate them. There is no statute of limitations on the recovery of such materials, and there should be no exceptions.

2) State laws that "declare" that what was once possibly a public record is again a public record are *wrong*. States pass those laws for the sole purpose of justifying "grabs" of selective items in private hands.

3) If a collector, dealer, or institution can show that items have been publicly bought and sold *and* that he or she or it is a *bona fide* owner of the item(s), a state

or municipality would be under a strict obligation to verify with hard evidence that the item was stolen. A state should not be allowed, after a decades of public lethargy and silence, to confiscate items that have been outside the archives in public view.

4) Items that have been openly bought, sold, traded, and/or featured in articles should be immune from confiscation if an archives cannot prove theft or misappropriation. When a state or institution seeks to reclaim allegedly stolen or misappropriated materials, there must be proof that the items were once held in a state repository and then stolen or misappropriated.

5) Collectors should be sensitive to a state's desire to fill in the blanks of its history. If the archives will accept a copy, the dealer or collector should provide it.

6) Real estate law provides for an action to "quiet title" on property claimed by competing interests. A quiet title action establishes one party's title, and thus "quiets" any challenges or claims to the title. An action to quiet a title requires description of the property in question and names anyone who might have an interest and the factual and legal basis for their claims. Published notice goes out to all potentially interested parties. The court's decision quiets and provides a legal "good title." In the spirit of the quiet title process, states should be encouraged to advertise its missing materials when they discover them missing.[31]

Petersen sums up his argument by asking, "Why—after years of inaction and silence—should a state be allowed to pass confiscatory legislation to summarily claim items to which it simply 'declares' its ownership. This is tantamount to eminent domain on personal property."[32]

In an email conversation among several Manuscript Society members, Petersen defined what he would accept as "proof" that a document came out of an archives illegally. He wrote that he would want to know "that the government has maintained all similar records. If the government cannot show a pattern of maintaining its manuscript records, then the presumption should work against the state and in favor of the collector, dealer or institution."[33] In other words, the law could presume that, in the absence of records to the contrary, the government had legally relinquished the materials. Petersen elaborated further by arguing that "even if it can be proven to be a state record—if the item's provenance shows it has been trafficked in public offerings and sales over a period of years—without the state ever saying 'boo,' the equitable doctrine of *laches* should apply."[34]

Another party in the email conversation, George Vogt, who had served as the Director of the South Carolina Department of Archives between 1987 and 1996, argued that "the public records of a government [cannot] be made into private property, except by formal deaccession, no matter how much time has elapsed."[35] Petersen responded, "What exactly is 'formal deaccession'? And have the standards of today been followed 25, 50, 100, 200 years ago? You would put the burden on the dealer/collector to prove that the item was not stolen rather than [on the state to prove] that it was. Where there is evidence indeed that an item

WAS stolen, I think we would all be in agreement. However, not everything is black & white and we need to worry about a whole lot of grey!"[36]

Vogt replied, "I'll stipulate that some states have been asses about replevin, but I won't agree to the idea that states must prove theft. The collections are far too large to maintain item control, so things 'disappear' unaccountably only to emerge years later in the marketplace." [37] Recall that the combined holdings for all state archives in 2006 amounted to more than 2.7 million cubic feet up from just under 1.8 million cubic feet a decade earlier, and growing at around 100,000 cubic feet each year. Further recall that a 2004 CoSA survey found that in 16 state archives "50% or more of their holdings were described at only the most basic level, e.g., title, dates, and quantity."[38] Across all the archives, 37 percent had their holdings described at this basic level, "41% at a midlevel that includes some information about creator and content, and about 19% at a detailed level."[39]

Vogt continued, "Many of the Lincoln scribbles and notes that are [on the market] were comments pinned by himself to federal documents and, presumably, unpinned and pocketed years later. These are technically part of the federal record, but NARA would probably not go after something minor like that unless an earlier microfilm showed the item still pinned to the record. But there are plenty of things [on the market] that clearly, clearly were part of the state or federal record at some time."[40]

How would a state "prove" that something was stolen? Vogt mentions microfilm showing that the archives once held the documents. Petersen mentioned the existence of a long run of similar records from the same era. CoSA suggests that detailed descriptions make identifying specific items possible.

Other Issues

Presidential Libraries

The tradition of creating a library dedicated to the life and presidency of a former President of the United States started with Franklin D. Roosevelt. Thirteen presidents, from Hoover through George W. Bush, now have one. While each of these libraries receives its funding from private foundations created to support that particular library, NARA manages them all. All the libraries contain both records and private papers documenting the life before, during, and after the presidency. Wanting to develop as complete a collection as possible, these repositories collect both incoming and outgoing correspondence. Incoming correspondence falls under the heading of a public record; outgoing correspondence does not. What might the curator in one of these libraries properly use the power of replevin to acquire? Although I find no record of their actually using the power of replevin to gather in documents, I have heard anecdotal evidence that some have used the threat of replevin to pressure people to "donate" private papers to them.

Retiring Public Officials

Many states, as well as the federal government, have laws that direct retiring executive branch officials on where they should deposit their papers. Regardless, however, public officials deposit all or some in other repositories—frequently university Special Collections. Archivists think that all executive branch records of enduring value should go into the archives, and many have tried to make that the law; most have not succeeded.[41]

What about Copies?

While collectors and dealers have no interest in copies, archivists have a long history of accepting and working with copies. In his 1939 study of archival practice in state archives, SAA president Albert Newsome found that "thirty-five states have made legal provision for the restoration of lost, missing or destroyed archives such as records of deeds, wills, mortgages, judgments and other instruments. Restoration is made by rerecording the original or a certified copy and by *ex parte* proceedings by depositions, affidavits and witnesses."[42] Roughly ten years later, Morris Leon Radoff, second archivist of Maryland, wrote, "We have learned in Maryland to face the bitter truth that early records have become a commodity for which there is active demand—they go to the highest bidders.... There is little to be gained by deploring the past. Let those institutions which have records of their neighbors return them if they wish, but let us remember that they were bought with hard money, raised with difficulty, or were bequeathed along with provisions that they be kept perpetually. Ask for photocopies or microfilm copies and fill as many gaps as possible. Does it make any real difference where the original is to be found?"[43] Having said that in print, however, he systematically charmed original records from county clerks "by promising to replace the originals with high-quality photostats."[44]

In 1981, Frank Burke, Executive Director of the NHPRC from 1975 to 1988, Acting Archivist of the United States from April 16, 1985, to December 4, 1987, and former professor of archives administration at the University of Maryland, mused, "What is the difference between information and the medium on which the information has been inscribed?.... Do archivists confuse the artifact value of their documents with artifact values in museums and art galleries? Is the nature of information such that man will be satisfied to receive it in surrogate form, and not care if the original is discarded? Why do we retain originals when copies have been made; and, at some point in time, should original documents that have been copied be transferred to museum to be treated as craft artifacts, while the archivist remains concerned only with the information from the documents, which has been suitably transformed into a more useable form?"[45] Collectors would answer, "Yes!"

James O'Toole tracks archivists' relationship to original documents. He argues that archivists readily accepted copies because they understood that they could not ensure the survival of originals, largely because of the threat of fire. By the mid-twentieth century, central heating systems all but eliminated the threat fire once posed, and archival theory began to focus on the "inherent value" of original documents. O'Toole cited an article published in *American Archivist* as instrumental in making that shift, but evidence suggests that the article merely reflected a shift in the attitude of practicing archivists.[46]

For example, by 1961, Maryland's Morris Radoff had modified his 1948 position. He had become keenly aware that Maryland records, such as those in the custody of the Library of Congress and the Maryland Historical Society, had left Maryland from unguarded depositories, often under the eyes of indifferent custodians; some of the custodians themselves had perpetrated the thefts. Regardless, he maintained that the records of a government belong to that government. Unless the government voluntarily divests itself of title, it owns the records no matter how far and for how long they have strayed.[47]

When Quincey Mumford, the Librarian of Congress, refused to surrender its Maryland holdings, Radoff used Congressional pressure to persuade him to return them. Mumford returned them, on "indefinite loan."[48] On another occasion, Radoff fixed his eye on the Scharf Collection at the Maryland Historical Society. J. Thomas Scharf, had served as a commissioner of the Land Office of Maryland. As collector of Maryland historical materials and as custodian of many of the records of the state, he tended to confuse his two roles. In 1900, the report of the Public Archives Commission stated that "many early Maryland documents seem to have disappeared in connection with the research of Scharf, the historian of the state." It is suspected that he actively peddled state records to private individuals, lost others through inattention, gave others away, and finally took what he wanted. Radoff wanted the papers for the state archives. The Maryland Historical Society (MHS) maintained "that the deed of gift"[49] prevented that. "But the Historical Society never refused permission to copy the materials."[50] When Radoff learned that the MHS would allow the archives to make copies, he decided not to sue for the originals. "Replevin is a dangerous method to use in recovering manuscripts," he stated, "because it makes for the disappearance of records or their sale outside the state. Further, it endangers institutions like the Maryland Historical Socitey[*sic*] which had procured them honestly by purchase or bequest years ago."[51]

Moreover, as technology improved and space diminished, archivists embraced the value of copies. In 1975, federal law allowed copies of documents to serve as evidence, provided there was no question about the authenticity of the copy. "The original is never required if the original is lost or destroyed. Thus, originals can be microfilmed and destroyed and the microfilm copy would be admissible as if it were the destroyed original."[52]

As part of an SAA session panel in 2008, archivist Elena S. Danielson opined that out of concern for the integrity of disputed document or collection, rather than break it up for distribution to disputing parties, a creative solution could involve copies.[53] Another member of the same panel, attorney Tim Ingram, asked about how to decide on how much to spend fighting over estrayed documents. He allowed that if they have much value (undefined), they may be worth fighting over, but he questioned it otherwise. He also raised the issue of who decides what to copy and pays for the selection and copying itself.[54]

As a general rule, archivists have a legal obligation to maintain a complete historical record. To quote John Fleckner again, "As archivists who maintain the integrity of the historical record, we guard our collective past from becoming the mere creation of 'official history.'"[55] That's a high calling, and they take it seriously. In some cases, legislation requires that they preserve the original document. California serves as an example. As I wrote in the previous chapter, if a person, organization, or institution returns a document to the California archives, "the secretary or a local agency that receives the record shall issue to that person, organization, or institution a copy or digital image of the record, which shall be certified as a true copy of the record that was returned to the state or local agency, and dated on the same day the record was returned."[56] Other archives don't have a legal requirement that they accept only the original, but they all prefer the original document.

The archivist of one of those states told me that the archives can't accept copies because a copy isn't the public record and so it doesn't satisfy the law. Since he cannot accept copies, he admitted that deciding what to pursue involves a lot of factors, including market value, but he has no firm line in the value of something that triggers the state's going after it.

I see right on both sides of this dispute. I hope you do as well as you address the cases that follow.

Notes

1. James B. Rhoads, "Alienation and Thievery: Archival Problems," *American Archivist* 29 (April 1966): 199.

2. Oliver Metzger, "Making the Doctrine of *res extra commercium* Visible in United States Law," *Texas Law Review 74* (February 1996): 615.

3. "Historical Writings: The Independent Value of Possession," *Yale Law Review* 67 (Nov. 1957): 160.

4. The Free Dictionary, http://legal-dictionary.thefreedictionary.com/laches (Jan. 3, 2011).

5. Metzger, "Making the doctrine of *res extra commercium* Visible."

6. "So You Want to Be an Archivist: An Overview of the Archives Profession," http://www2.archivists.org/profession (Jan. 3, 2011).

7. J. Frank Cook, "The Blessings of Providence on an Association of Archivists," *American Archivist* 46 (Fall 1983): 399.

8. John Fleckner. "'Dear Mary Jane': Some Reflections on Being an Archivist," *American Archivist* 54 (Winter 1991): 12.

9. Michigan Department of History, Archives, and Libraries, "eBay and Archival Collections," http://www.michigan.gov/hal/0,1607,7-160-15479-127674--,00.html (Oct. 25, 2009).

10. Michigan, "eBay and Archival Collections."

11. Council of State Archivists, *The State of State Records: A Status Report on State Archives and Records Management Programs in the United States* (Iowa City, Iowa: Council of State Archivists, 2007), 11, http://www.statearchivists.org/reports/2007ARMreport (April 15, 2011).

12. For the full story, see http://www.tampabay.com/news/humaninterest/she-has-davy-crocketts-marriage-license-and-isnt-giving-it-up/1062408 or http://www.pbs.org/wgbh/roadshow/archive/200502A20.html or http://www.museum-security.org/?p=3826 (April 23, 2011).

13. Council of State Archivists, *The State of State Records*, 10.

14. Council of State Archivists, *The State of State Records*, 20.

15. James E. O'Neill, "Replevin: A Public Archivist's Perspective," *College and Research Libraries* 40 (January 1979): 30.

16. No one has taken up the question of how web-based publication of privately held public documents might fit into this discussion.

17. Richard Maass, "Arguments Heard in the Clark Case," *Manuscripts* 8 (Winter 1956): 113–116.

18. Kenneth Rendell in an email to the author with the subject "RE: For your consideration" (May 30, 2011).

19. Kenneth Rendell in an email to the author with the subject "RE: Quoting you," (June 16, 2011).

20. "D.A.R. Desires Virginia to Take Action to Recover Martha Washington's Will," *New York Times*, Jan. 7, 1914, 2.

21. Michael H. Harris, *History of Libraries of the Western World (*Metuchen, N.J.: Scarecrow Press, 1995), 267; "Library of Congress" brochure, 2. See also, John L. Smithmeyer, *History of the Construction of the Library of Congress, Washington, D.C.* (Washington, D.C.: Beresford, 1906). For a detailed description of the floor plan for the Library of Congress, see Library of Congress, *Report of the Librarian of Congress, 1897* (Washington, D.C.: Government Printing Office, 1897).

22. Aaron D. Purcell, "Abstractions of Justice: The Library of Congress's Great Manuscripts Robbery, 1896–1897," *American Archivist* 62 (Fall 1999): 327.

23. Purcell, "Abstractions of Justice," 328.

24. Purcell. "Abstractions of Justice," 328; Fred Shelley, "Manuscripts in the Library of Congress: 1800–1900," *American Archivist* 11 (January 1948): 6, 7, 11–12; Robert H. Laud, "Defense of Archives Against Human Foes," *American Archivist* 19 (April 1956): 127–28.

25. Purcell, "Abstractions of Justice," 329.

26. Purcell, "Abstractions of Justice," 329; Land, "Defense of Archives," 127; Library of Congress Archives, "Statement of Lewis McKenzie Turner," 27, 30–32.

27. Purcell, "Abstractions of Justice," 339.

28. Purcell, "Abstractions of Justice," 340.

29. Email among Scott Petersen and leaders in the Manuscript Society: Edward N. Bomsey, George L. Vogt, Anthony J. Mourek, and Ivo Meisner, subject "Replevin" (Jan. 4, 2006).

30. Scott Petersen, in a personal conversation with the author, spring, 2010.

31. Scott Petersen, "Another Perspective on Replevin," *Rail Splitter* 10 (Summer/Fall 2004): 10.

32. Scott Peteresen, Unpublished draft of "Another Perspective on Replevin," *Rail Splitter* 10 (Summer/Fall 2004). In the author's possession.

33. Email among Scott Petersen and leaders in the Manuscript Society: Edward N. Bomsey, George L. Vogt, Anthony J. Mourek, and Ivo Meisner, subject "RE: Replevin," (Jan. 4, 2006).

34. Email among Scott Petersen and leaders in the Manuscript Society: Edward N. Bomsey, George L. Vogt, Anthony J. Mourek, and Ivo Meisner, subject "RE: Replevin," (Jan. 4, 2006).

35. Email among Scott Petersen and leaders in the Manuscript Society: Edward N. Bomsey, George L. Vogt, Anthony J. Mourek, and Ivo Meisner, subject "RE: Replevin," (Jan. 4, 2006).

36. Email among Scott Petersen and leaders in the Manuscript Society: Edward N. Bomsey, George L. Vogt, Anthony J. Mourek, and Ivo Meisner, subject "RE: Replevin," (Jan. 4, 2006).

37. For more on the size of state collections see, Council of State Archivists, *The State of State Records*, 25.

38. Council of State Archivists, *The State of State Records*, 33.

39. Council of State Archivists, *The State of State Records*, 34.

40. Email among Scott Petersen and leaders in the Manuscript Society: Edward N. Bomsey, George L. Vogt, Anthony J. Mourek, and Ivo Meisner, subject "RE: Replevin," (Jan. 4, 2006).

41. Paul Grondahl, "Records from Governors are Slow in Coming," *TimesUnion. Com* (June 12, 2011), http://www.timesunion.com/local/article/Records-from-governors-are-slow-in-coming-1420344.php (June 17, 2011).

42. Albert Ray Newsome, "Uniform State Archival Legislation," *American Archivist* 2 (January 1939): 11.

43. Marcia Talley, "Morris Leon Radoff: The Man and the Monument," *American Archivist* 44 (Fall 1981): 331.

44. Talley, "Morris Leon Radoff," 329.

45. Frank G. Burke, "The Future Course of Archival Theory in the United States," *American Archivist* 44 (Winter 1981): 44.

46. James O'Toole, "On the Idea of Permanence," *American Archivist* 51 (Winter 1989): 10–25; he referenced William J. Barrow, "Deacidification and Lamination of Deteriorated Documents, 1938–1963," *American Archivist* 28 (April 1965): 285.

47. Talley, "Morris Leon Radoff," 331–332.

48. Talley, "Morris Leon Radoff," 333.

49. The contract between the donor and the MHS through which the donor turned ownership over to the MHS.

50. Talley, "Morris Leon Radoff," 332–333.

51. Talley, "Morris Leon Radoff," 333.

52. Gary M. Peterson and Trudy Huskamp Peterson, *Archives and Manuscripts: Law* (Chicago: Society of American Archivists, 1985), 89, http://www2.archivists.org/sites/all/files/Archives&Mss-Law.pdf (April 24, 2011).

53. Elena S. Danielson, panelist for "Returning Displaced Archives," SAA Annual Meeting 2008, Session 405.

54. Tim Ingram, panelist for "Returning Displaced Archives," SAA Annual Meeting 2008, Session 405.

55. Fleckner, "'Dear Mary Jane,'" 12.

56. California, Section 1, Chapter 3.01 (commencing with Section 6204) is added to Division 7 of Title 1 of the Government Code California. Official California Legislative Information, www.leginfo.ca.gov/pub/09-10/bill/asm/ab_1201-1250/ab_1245_bill_20091011_chaptered.html (Jan. 4, 2010).

Chapter 7

Case Studies

Reading about an issue like replevin will take you only so far. To really understand, you have to grapple with a real-world application of the theories involved, including all the messiness the real world usually entails. I have created these case studies so you can do just that.

Generalities about Public Documents

As the various examples in chapter 5 indicate, governments differ in their definition of public documents. However, we can make some generalizations. Government archivists do not consider government-created documents intended for distribution to individual members or organizations in society to be public documents. By comparison, government archivists regard as public documents those created by a governmental body and intended for its own use and keeping. So, licenses, commissions, deeds, and outgoing mail do not fall under the definition of public documents, but records of the granting of licenses, records of commissions granted, indexes to deeds, incoming letters, and other documents recorded by governmental clerks and retained by them do fall under that definition. That category also includes ledgers recording the official business of a governmental body, minutes of meetings, charters or records of organization, ordinances, etc. It will also include records of poor farms, jails, public hospitals, reform schools, and public schools.

However, although a document meets the definition of public document, it may not have archival value. Governments archive only about 2.5–5 percent of potential archival materials; they destroy the rest. Although government archivists generally agree on what has archival value, they don't have perfect overlap in their collections; each state appraises its own materials for archival value using its own standard.

The Stage and the Players

Because the laws and rules that govern archival materials vary so widely, I've created three different states with three different sets of rules and laws. While I've set each case within a particular state so you can work with it in that context, I encourage you to work with the same circumstances in one or both of the different states. Or, just move one of the players to a different state and play with the possibilities. You will quickly see how complicated the whole topic becomes.

The State of Softline

Records Definition

The State of Softline defines public documents as a document created or received in the performance of a public duty or paid for by public funds by a governing body; public records belong to the public as public property.

Records Authority

Softline gives the State Archivist the responsibility of determining which state records belong in the archives in their original format, which records the state will destroy or otherwise dispose of after microfilming, and which records the state will destroy or otherwise dispose of without microfilming. The law, written in the mid-twentieth century, says nothing about private ownership of archival records.

Legal Position

In Softline the legal position on items that may have been stolen tends toward the concept that unless the archives can prove previous ownership, the accused owns the property.

The State of Midline

Records Definition

The State of Midline defines public documents as any writing containing information relating to the conduct of the public's business prepared, owned, used, or retained by a state or local agency regardless of physical form or characteristics. Hardline excludes from that definition the extra copies of printed or processed material that it may have retained.

Records Authority

Midline gives the State Archivist the responsibility of determining which state records belong in the archives in their original format, which records they will destroy or otherwise dispose of after microfilming, and which records the state will destroy or otherwise dispose of without microfilming. Midline public records laws make very clear that their records cannot be legally held by another party without a repository agreement from the Midline Archives. If a person, organization, or institution returns a Midline document, the State Archivist will issue to that person, organization, or institution a certified and dated true copy or digital image of the record that was returned. The law says nothing about accepting copies.

Legal Position

In Midline, the legal position on items that may have been stolen tends toward the concept that if the archives can show probable ownership through circumstantial evidence, the accused must relinquish the property.

State of Hardline

Records Definition

The State of Hardline defines public documents as all documentary material, regardless of media or characteristics, made or received in the transaction of its official business and maintained by an agency in accordance with law. It declares that all laws about public records are retrospective and retroactive, incorporating common law, colonial law, and early state statutes regarding the preservation of public records.

Records Authority

Hardline uses records retention schedules to determine what records go to the archives and which go to a records center to await shredding. The law specifically says that the destruction of records must occur only according to an approved retention schedule. The records retention schedule also determines which state records belong in the archives in their original format, which records the state will destroy or otherwise dispose of after microfilming, and which records the state will destroy or otherwise dispose of without microfilming. It further holds that a public record can never become a private record and makes illegal any private ownership of any public document. Hardline explicitly forbids the separation of any public record from public ownership and gives the State Archivist the authority to initiate legal action against anyone who holds public records to retrieve the original documents. The State Archivist may not accept copies.

Legal Position

In Hardline, the legal position on items that may have been stolen tends toward the concept that if the archives can show probable ownership through circumstantial evidence, the accused must relinquish the property.

Autograph Dealers and a Collector

Trusty Dealer

The dealer has owned a modest autograph and manuscripts business on the outskirts of the state's capital city for 25 years. Over that time he has built a large clientele of trusted sources and buyers. Very discrete and scrupulously honest, he believes honesty has built his business, which depends very much on trust. He and his clients have a very high level of trust in each other. Collectors and other dealers all know that he has developed a deep understanding of the nuances of replevin issues, and they routinely ask him for his opinion—which he gives freely.

Indifferent (Indy) Dealer

This is Trusty's younger brother. Indy does not share Trusty's meticulous ways. He argues that there's enough "good stuff" around that you don't need to rely on customer loyalty. He also argues that if something is on the market, it must be fair game, and he doesn't concern himself with provenance.

Ardent Collector

This collector caught the collecting bug early on and has never lost his passion. He has never really settled on a particular collecting focus; instead, his interests tend to evolve over time. Although he collects more than he sells, he funds part of his collecting by selling selected items or portions of his collection from time to time. He acquires materials in many ways (he *loves* auctions), from many sources. He has dealt with Trusty Dealer for decades and trusts him absolutely. Occasionally he trades with Indy Dealer, but only cautiously.

The State Archivists

The three states each have a State Archivist. To keep the attitudes and resources consistent across the states, I've created one personality with three names—one for each of the states—Sophisticated (Sophie) Archivist for the state of Softline; Meritorious (Meri) Archivist for Midline; and Hildegarde (Hilda) Archivist for Hardline. The difference in the cases won't depend on the difference in the State Archivist, although in real life, the personality of the State Archivist would play a role.

Sophie/Meri/Hilda Archivist has a double master's degree—one in history and one in library science with an archives management specialization. She became head of the state archives as her third career move and has had the position for about ten years. She has dealt with replevin only occasionally in the past ten years, but she has worked with her Attorney General's office on other matters. Any requests for archival records she gets from the AG's office get top priority from her and her staff.

Sophie/Meri/Hilda knows that dealers and collectors respond to discovering a stolen document in their possession in one of three ways: 1) Some won't cooperate even when they know a document belongs in a state archives. 2) Some will bend over backward to help recover a stolen document. 3) Some will cooperate only when contacted by law enforcement. Sophie/Meri/Hilda finds that out-of-state dealers and collectors may refuse to comply with a request to return materials, while in-state dealers generally do comply. When asked, some dealers will remove an item from an auction and agree to keep the items safe until archives personnel can pick it up. Other dealers, especially those who run online auctions, just broker sales—they do not have the item in hand and cannot return it. Sophie/Meri/Hilda has had cases where the dealer serves as the liaison for her archives and the holder of a state document, leading to the deposit of the document in the archives as a charitable contribution. She has no way of knowing how often public documents have changed hands through private negotiations and sales; she tries not to think about it.

Sophie/Meri/Hilda has found that the Internet actually improves the likelihood that the archives will learn of estrayed documents' being sold. She has an organization, the Friends of the Archives, that works on the archives behalf in many ways. Some members collect manuscripts themselves, and as they look for materials for their own collections, they spot state materials and notify her. The Friends also occasionally raise money to help her retrieve alienated materials.

Sophie/Meri/Hilda uses her institutional website to announce missing materials as a sort of "proof" that the archives owned something and knows that it's missing. To make that point stronger, she always files a missing documents report with the police. She also runs a tight ship. Every researcher must fill out a form giving an extensive amount of contact information. The people who serve the researcher use that form to create an inventory of all the materials they provide the researcher to work with. Sophie/Meri/Hilda then files these researcher records in case something goes missing; the researcher record tells her which researcher used the materials. She has also instituted a requirement that no staff member, including herself, may work in the stacks alone. Everyone finds the policy inconvenient, but they also understand that it keeps them above suspicion of theft.

Sophie/Meri/Hilda has never made a claim on a document that she was not sure would stand up in court. She would prefer not to take people to court and will do what she can to make the return of documents as mutually beneficial as possible for the donor as her laws allow. She has several ways of softening the blow: she can arrange for an independent appraisal to place a market value on returned materials so the donor can take a tax deduction for the "donation"; she has staged homecoming events to celebrate the return of estrayed materials; she has even repaid a holder for the cost of conservation treatments she or he had done. If, however, she must go to court, she will provide her AG the best evidence and arguments she can to support her claim.

In the pages below, the first section deals with simple examples of determining what is and what is not considered a public document. The more complex second section presents a series of hypothetical cases based on real-world situations. Although the contexts come from a variety of sources as well as my imagination, the issues reflect the experiences that archivists, collectors, and dealers encounter on a routine basis.

Part I. Recognizing a Public Document

1. Trusty Dealer got an email from Ardent Collector. Ardent said he has an August 2, 1939, autograph letter signed from Albert Einstein, scientist, to Franklin Delano Roosevelt, President of the United States, proposing the government build a nuclear bomb. Ardent asked Trusty if he may sell it as a private document. What should Trusty tell Ardent?

2. Trusty Dealer got an email from Ardent Collector. Ardent said he has two original New York State driver's licences issued to and signed by Jacqueline Kennedy Onassis. Ardent asked Trusty if he may sell them as private documents. What should Trusty tell Ardent?

3. Trusty Dealer got an email from Ardent Collector. Ardent said he has an Abraham Lincoln note to Secretary of War Edwin Stanton dated April 10, 1865. Lincoln writes, "Tad[1] wants some flags. Can he be accommodated?" Ardent asked if he may sell it as a private document. What should Trusty tell Ardent?

4. Trusty Dealer got an email from Ardent Collector. Ardent said he has the letter Harry Truman wrote the music reviewer of the *Washington Post* on December 6, 1950, berating the reviewer for a poor review he gave a concert that Margaret Truman had presented. Ardent asked if he may sell it as a private document. What should Trusty tell Ardent?

5. Trusty Dealer got an email from Ardent Collector. Ardent said he has a printed letter signed by Theodore Roosevelt as President, December 25, 1908, to Louisa Lee Schuyler, Vice President of the State Charities Aid Association. The letter invited her to attend a conference on the federal government's interest in child welfare matters. Ardent asked if he may sell it as a private document. What should Trusty tell Ardent?

6. Trusty Dealer got an email from Ardent Collector. Ardent said he has an autographed letter signed by J. Q. Adams as a Member of the House of Representatives, dated October 2, 1837. It is written to John S. Tyler of Boston, a constituent. Adams had asked the Commissioner of Pensions whether the Massachusetts roll may furnish evidence of Tyler's grandfather's service in the Revolutionary War and enclosed his own memories of Tyler's grandfather. Ardent asked if he may sell it as a private document. What should Trusty tell Ardent?

7. Trusty Dealer got an email from Ardent Collector. Ardent said he has Paul Revere's expense statement to the Boston Committee of Public Safety to cover his January 3, 1774, ride from Boston to New York and Philadelphia to spread news of the Boston Tea Party. Ardent asked if he may sell it as a private document. What should Trusty tell Ardent?

8. Trusty Dealer got an email from Ardent Collector. Ardent explained that on December 23, 1783, George Washington went before the Continental Congress to resign his commission as Commander-in-Chief of the Continental Army. He submitted his written resignation and accompanied it with brief and very moving remarks. As he left the Old Senate Chamber to return to Mt. Vernon, he handed his personal copy of the remarks to a member of the committee that had arranged the ceremony. The document has remained within that family, which now wants to sell it to him privately. Ardent asked if he may buy it as a private document. What should Trusty tell Ardent?

Part II. The Cases

In the cases below, the characters move from state to state. The state they represent in each case will appear in parentheses after their names. Trusty Dealer dominated Part I, but he doesn't appear much in Part II. In the real world, most dealers resemble Trusty: they scrupulously avoid anything that seems "too good to be true" or looks like a public document. The annals of manuscripts theft abound with tales of dealers sensing something amiss about something they've been offered—perhaps they recognize a public document and return it to its proper archives, or perhaps they alert the archives of a public document's appearance on the market. Being caught dealing with stolen or public materials has no upside; most dealers understand that the news will hurt them personally, professionally, and financially.

That's the real world. But to have case studies one must have conflict, so Indy Dealer dominates the cases. Indy represents a small minority of dealers, but he exists and he causes a lot of grief to the world of archives and collectors—as you will see.

1. Governor's Papers

Trusty Dealer (Softline) got a phone call one day from a man saying he had just finished cleaning out the family home and had some documents he wanted to sell. When the seller arrived with the materials in hand, Trusty recognized a rich array of correspondence from various officers in the Office of the Governor of Hardline to their counterparts in the Office of the Governor of Softline. Most discuss campus demonstrations protesting the Vietnam War. It appears that the two offices regularly exchanged strategies for responding to the demonstrations—collaboration Trusty had not heard of. Trusty immediately thought of them as public documents, but they had none of the usual stamps one would expect on incoming correspondence. Could they be forgeries? Could a family member have worked in a clerical position in the Governor's Office and intercepted them, photocopied them, and distributed the copies? The seller didn't say anything except that he had found them in the attic at the old house and he wondered if they might have some value.

What should Trusty do? Whom should he contact? What questions should he ask? Should he accept the letters?

2. Revolutionary Era Wills

Trusty Dealer (Midline) has done business with R.W. Collector for years; R.W. collects anything relating to the Revolutionary War era. Now getting up in years, R.W. has begun to sell off his collection—usually at the rate of one or two items a month. One day R.W. appears in Trusty's office with a briefcase full of eighteenth-century wills he wants to sell, all signed by prominent Revolutionary War era Virginians. Trusty prides himself on knowing what has bought and sold over the past few decades, and while he recognizes the names and signatures on the documents, he has no memory of any of these documents. Trusty asks R.W. about them, and R.W. tells him that his great-grandfather got out them of a courthouse during his service in the Union Army during the Civil War. In fact, they started R.W.'s interest in collecting Revolutionary War materials, but he's ready to let them go.

What should Trusty do? Whom should he contact? What questions should he ask? Should he accept the wills?

3. Penitentiary Ledger

Sally Hansen (Hardline) needed money. She had lost her job as a line worker in the local factory during the deep recession of the Bush and Obama administrations. She felt very fortunate that she and her late husband had paid off the mortgage and set a little aside. She could live on her widow's benefits and make ends meet, but if she wanted anything extra, she had to find a creative way to pay for it.

Sally had married Frank Hansen fairly late in life. He was a police officer when she met him, but in the 1970s he had started his career as a guard in the old nineteenth-century Hardline Penitentiary; he helped close the place. After they were married, Frank had shown her a book from the prison, a nineteenth-century ledger recording the names, physical descriptions, and crimes of incoming prisoners, as well as their date of release, transfer, or demise. She thought it was cool; he thought it might be worth something. Frank had died in the line of duty in 2006, and Sally had hung onto the book as a memento. Recently, however, she decided to sell it. She posted it to an online auction.

Hardline did close its nineteenth-century penitentiary in the 1970s. While the administration moved the prisoners efficiently enough, nobody paid much attention to the set of three nineteenth-century ledgers of prisoners. Volumes 1 and 3 went to the state archives, but volume 2 remained at large. One of Hilda Archivist's (Hardline) Friends group, monitoring online auctions, sales catalogs, and online classified sales, spotted the book almost as soon as Sally posted it and notified Hilda.

The auction site would not stop the sale, but it did provide Hilda with Sally's contact information. Hilda called Sally and explained that the ledger belonged to the state. She asked Sally when someone from the archives could come pick up the volume.

Questions to consider:

Is this a public document? Is there any evidence that an archives ever held it? What's the historical value? Can the State Archivist prove that it was stolen? Can the holder prove the right to hold it? What negotiating latitude do the state laws give the State Archivist? What negotiable solutions can you think of; what can the State Archivist do; what can the holder do? How would this case be different if the State Archivist and the holder did not live in the same state? How would this case be different if they both lived in one of the other states?

4. Cut Pages

Sophie Archivist (Softline) sat at her computer using a search engine to answer a researcher's request for background material on a Revolutionary War general. She discovered, in the process, that Indifferent Dealer (Midline) just sold what appeared to be several pages from a 1777–1778 government auditor's ledger the Softline archives holds. Upon checking the ledger, Sophie discovered the pages had been cut out of the book, and upon checking the researcher records, discovered that a thief who was recently convicted for stealing numerous documents from various repositories in the late 1980s had worked with the auditor's ledger. She could not tell what the pages held that made them so attractive.

Sophie contacted Indy Dealer, who refused to reveal either for whom he had brokered the stolen documents or to whom he had sold them. Indy, however, contacted the buyer and reported back to Sophie that his buyer told him the documents had been sold again. Sophie knew that, even if she took legal action against Indy to obtain the name of the buyer, she would need to pursue that buyer in a separate legal action. She asked her Attorney General to press the case, but the pages had a relatively low market value and would cost more to pursue than their market value warranted. Further, Indy Dealer did not live in Softline. The AG refused. What can Sophie do?

Questions to consider:

Are these public documents? What historical value do they have? What negotiating latitude do the state laws give the State Archivist? What negotiable solutions can you think of; what can the State Archivist do; what can the holder do? How would this case be different if the State Archivist and the holder did not live in the same state? How would this case be different if they both lived in one of the other states?

5. Tracking Stolen Documents

Trusty Dealer (Midline) just returned two documents to Meri Archivist (Midline). The archives' researcher records indicate that the documents probably walked out about eight years earlier. Meri suspects the same thief stole them both and may have taken other material; she decided to track the documents back to the thief. Although the thief himself had died several years ago, Meri obtained the name of the Hardline dealer who had sold the documents for him, and she went to Hardline's capital city to meet him. She found the dealer suffering from advanced dementia and his family in the middle of liquidating all of his holdings. The family told Meri that his business records of the past 10 years were incomprehensible. Further, they did not want to slow down their process to allow her try to sort through the records, even if it would mean that she might identify additional documents stolen from her collections. What might Meri do?

Questions to consider:

What negotiable solutions can you think of; what can the State Archivist do; what can the family do?

6. Court Record

Agnes Gooch lived in a trailer park in South Midline. She had lost her home and most of her belonging in the mortgage crisis of 2008–2009. Her ex-brother-in-law had allowed her to live in his trailer for a modest rent. She could not find work, and had decided to sell an old book she inherited from her father. The book, a court record book for Midline County, 1717–1733, was completely intact and in beautiful shape; her father had had a conservator tighten its bindings at one time. For some reason he left the invoice for the work in the book.

Agnes called the Midline County Historical Society (MCHS) and asked if it would buy the book. The fellow she talked with gave her a vague answer about needing to talk with the Curator. He said he would get back to her. He then called Meri Archivist (Midline). Meri recognized the book immediately. She knew the archives held Midline County court record books from 1681–1709 and a complete set from 1733–1920, when the series ended; the archives did not have records between 1717 and 1733. Meri knew this book belonged in the collection and suspected it would complete the set.

When the phone rang, Agnes expected to hear from the MCHS, but instead she found a lawyer from the Midline State Archives saying he wanted to come get the book. Agnes sat down in despair; what could she do?

Questions to consider:

Is this a public document? Is there any evidence that an archives ever held it? What's the historical value? Can the State Archivist prove that it belongs in the archives? Can the holder prove the right to hold it? What negotiating latitude do the Midline state laws give the State Archivist? What negotiable solutions can you think of; what can the State Archivist do; what can the holder do? How would this case be different if the State Archivist and the holder did not live in the same state? How would this case be different if they both lived in one of the other states?

7. Colonial Guardianship Volumes

The books called Hardline's "Bonds of Guardianship," Volumes 1 through 4 (1830–1852), record the details of colonial and state guardianships through 1852. The first recorded information about guardianships in Hardline history, they hold important genealogical information. Ardent Collector (Softline) found the historic volumes at Softline Books, Softline City. Immediately recognizing these books as public records, Ardent contacted Hilda Archivist (Hardline).

When the book store owner got the call from the Hilda, she immediately resisted. She explained that she had bought the books for $200 each at the estate auction of one of Hardline's most prominent politicians. Why, she wondered aloud, if the state archives was so worried about missing public documents, didn't it sent someone to the auction?

After she had calmed down, the bookseller offered to sell the book to Hilda for 25 percent over the price she had paid. Alternatively, she would have them microfilmed if Hilda would pay for it, but she would not just give them back.

Questions to consider:

Are these public documents? What government do they document? Is there any evidence that an archives ever held it? What's the historical value? How can the State Archivist prove that they were stolen? How can the holder prove the right to hold it? What negotiating latitude do the applicable laws give the State Archivist? What negotiable solutions can you think of; what can the State Archivist do; what can the holder do? How would this case be different if they both lived in one of the other states?

8. Revolutionary War Generals

Meri Archivist (Midline) received the grandchildren of old Mrs. Laudable in her office; she remembered seeing the obituary in the paper a few months ago. Mrs. Laudable's descendants had come from a neighboring state to clean out her house so it could go on the market. They showed Meri several handwritten letters between two Revolutionary War generals (both ancestors of Mrs. L) debating the best way to carry out orders from higher up. The orders relate to a pivotal battle that took place in Midline when it was a wilderness area claimed by three competing colonies. The Laudable decedents wanted to know how much Meri would pay to add them to her holdings. They made clear that they intend to ask the same question to the Midline Historical Society and the National Park Service, which manages the battleground site. They will sell to the highest bidder.

Questions to consider:

Are these public documents? What government do they document? What's the historical value? What negotiating latitude do the applicable laws give the State Archivist? What negotiable solutions can you think of; what can the State Archivist do; what can the holder do? How would this case be different if the State

Archivist and the holder did not live in the same state? How would this case be different if they both lived in one of the other states?

9. Book of Surveys

At his direction, Indifferent Dealer's (Midline) nephew had picked up at auction a 1730 book of surveys that appeared to have established the lots and claims of the area that became Founderville, Midline. Indy had bought it, sight unseen, thinking it had come from Founderville, Softline. When he discovered the mistake, he put the book up for sale. Meri Archivist (Midline) had records showing that the book had been in the hands of the city government of Founderville, Midline, and contacted Indy. Indy offered to sell the book to Meri. Alternatively, he would have it microfilmed if Meri would pay for it, but he would not just give them back to her.

Questions to consider:

Is this a public document? What government does it document? Is there any evidence that an archives ever held it? What's the historical value? How can the State Archivist prove that it was stolen? How can the holder prove the right to hold it? What negotiating latitude do the applicable laws give the State Archivist? What negotiable solutions can you think of; what can the State Archivist do; what can the holder do? How would this case be different if the State Archivist and the holder did not live in the same state? How would this case be different if they both lived in one of the other states?

10. Letters Sold and Resold

Ardent Collector (Midline) had long ago bought—at a cost of several hundred dollars—correspondence between two very prominent early legislators as they forged the early laws of Midline during the state's first legislative session. The market's interest in these two men had gone up about tenfold, and Ardent decided to sell the letters. He posted them in an online auction, and before long he found himself facing Meri Archivist (Midline), who claimed that Ardent had no right to hold those public documents. Ardent was stunned! He knew these documents had been bought and sold on the open market at least back to the 1930s, and he had always assumed that the state had no interest in them. Meri explained that during the Great Depression, a clerk in the archives, with no authority to do so, had hired his brother-in-law to haul away old files to free up some space. Someone must have picked documents out of the dump and started selling them. Ardent held them illegally, and the archives expected him to give them back.

Incensed at the State Archivist's attitude, Ardent contacted a dealer friend in Softline and asked if he would like to buy the documents. The dealer friend said he would. Ardent then went to Meri and offered to sell her the letters one last time.

Questions to consider:

Are these public documents? Is there any evidence that an archives ever held them? What's the historical value? Can the State Archivist prove that they were stolen? Can the holder prove the right to hold it? What negotiating latitude do the state laws give the State Archivist? What negotiable solutions can you think of; what can the State Archivist do; what can the holder do? How would this case be different if the State Archivist and the holder did not live in the same state? How would this case be different if they both lived in one of the other states?

11. Retrieved from a Dump

In the 1960s, the State of Hardline launched a program to convert its nineteenth-century archival materials—except those with clear iconic value—to microfilm or microfiche. Since the project came from a need for more space, the program directive authorized the State Archivist to destroy (which in those days meant burn or dump) documents after filming. Word got out that the state was dumping old documents, and several enterprising dealers went to the dump and retrieved material they knew would sell. Ardent Collector bought several of those items and has now decided to sell them. No sooner had he posted them to an online auction than he found himself contacted by Hilda Archivist (Hardline) claiming them as public records. The archives could show that it had held them—it had the microfilm to prove it—but it had no record of having officially deaccessioned them. Ardent explained how he came to have them and expressed great exasperation that the State Archivist would challenge his right to have and sell them because it had not kept proper records of dumping them.

Questions to consider:

Are these public documents? What government do they document? Is there any evidence that an archives ever held it? What's the historical value? How can the State Archivist prove that it was stolen? How can the holder prove the right to hold it? What negotiating latitude do the applicable laws give the State Archivist? What negotiable solutions can you think of; what can the State Archivist do; what can the holder do? How would this case be different if it occurred in either of the other two states?

12. Town Clerk Miscellany

Indifferent Dealer (Softline), bought a box of documents at an estate sale for $150. As he expected, much of the contents had no commercial value, but he had bought box lots like this enough to know that somewhere he would find something. When he unfolded three different bundles at the bottom, he knew he had. The three bundles represented three different genres: letters written to government officials in Hardtown, applications for various Hardtown government-issued licences, and reports to various Hardtown officials about activities related to Depression-era internal improvement projects. Therefore, they contained many signatures of local citizens who had gained some historical importance within the state of Hardline.

Indy knew that an ancestor of the family that had sold off the estate had served as the Hardtown Town Clerk for 35 years in the nineteenth century, before the town built a government office building. The ancestor had his office in this home, and these bundles had escaped the move to the municipal building when it opened.

Indy had dealt with the archives in Hardline and understood very well its laws; he had no interest in attracting Hilda Archivist's attention on these, so he decided to sell them quickly and quietly to a handful of customers he knew would find them irresistible.

A week after the estate sale, one of the descendants of the Hardtown Town Clerk (an archives student) came home for a weekend. She heard all about the estate sale and the box of papers the family had sold. One of her cousins mentioned the bundles of letters, applications, and reports in it, and the archives student immediately understood that they belonged in the Hardline archives, which holds archival materials for local municipalities in the state. The student contacted the Hilda's office. Hilda contacted the auctioneer and asked who had purchased the item. The auctioneer wouldn't give her the information, but he offered to contact the buyer to see if he would sell them back to the auctioneer, who would then sell them to the archives. Hilda knew that, under the laws of Hardline, she could not pay for them, nor could she accept copies. She authorized the auctioneer to see if he could get the materials back. Immediately after, she contacted her Friends to see if they would raise the $150 to repay the auctioneer. She heard back from the auctioneer late that same afternoon; the buyers has already sold the documents to collectors out of state. When she got that answer, she sighed and went to the AG's office. She wanted them back.

Questions to consider:

Are these public documents? Is there any evidence that an archives ever held them? What's the historical value? Can the State Archivist prove that they were stolen? Can the holder prove the right to hold them? What negotiating latitude do the state laws give the State Archivist? What negotiable solutions can you think of; what can the State Archivist do; what can the holder do? How would this case be different if the State Archivist and the holder did not live in the same state? How would this case be different if they both lived in one of the other states?

13. Legendary Hero's Marriage License

Trusty Dealer (Hardline) received the granddaughter of Henry Hoarder. He had died recently and his granddaughter had come from a neighboring state to clean out his house so it could go on the market. She had found a marriage license among some old records; it had been signed by a native son who had become a national hero. The family wanted to sell it, and she asked Trusty if he would buy it for his inventory. Trusty asked what they knew about the document's provenance. She admitted that she had never seen it before, but she remembered her grandparents talking about it. It seems that her grandmother's grandfather had worked at the Hardcounty County courthouse during the Depression and he had told how he had found it in the trash one day. The Clerk of Courts had run out of room and threw out some really old records to make some shelf space. What should Trusty tell the granddaughter?

Questions to consider:

Is this a public document? Is there any evidence that an archives ever held it? What's the historical value? How can the State Archivist prove that it was stolen? How can the holder prove the right to hold it? What negotiating latitude do the applicable laws give the State Archivist? What negotiable solutions can you think of; what can the State Archivist do; what can the holder do? How would this case be different if the State Archivist and the holder did not live in the same state? How would this case be different if they both lived in one of the other states?

14. Governor's Commission Papers

Sophie Archivist (Softline) regularly attended meetings of the Society of Softline Archivists. As she drove home after the most recent meeting, she mulled over a conversation she had had with the Curator of Manuscripts at the Softline State University (SSU). The curator told her about an exciting new collection that had recently come to his repository. The family of a prominent, recently deceased, civic leader had given SSU her papers, including those from the time that she chaired Softline's first Governor's Commission on the Redress of Historical Grievances in the late 1960s and early 1970s. The SSU curator expressed a lot of enthusiasm because of the research potential the papers held for graduate students and faculty in several different disciplines. Sophie wondered if those papers didn't belong in the state archives.

Questions to consider:

Are these public documents? Is there any evidence that an archives ever held them? What's the historical value? Can the State Archivist prove that they were stolen? Can the holder prove the right to hold it? What negotiating latitude do the state laws give the State Archivist? What negotiable solutions can you think of; what can the State Archivist do; what can the holder do? How would this case be different if the State Archivist and the holder did not live in the same state? How would this case be different if they both lived in one of the other states?

15. Colonial Paymaster Ledger

Sophie Archivist (Softline) learned about the 1777 ledger kept by the Softline colonial militia paymaster being sold on an online auction site. Softline had a record showing that the archives had held the documents in its collection. Sophie contacted the legal department of an online auction site and asked that they stop the sale. The online auction administrators complied and supplied the name of the seller. The seller, a gentleman in Hardline, had bought the ledger as part of a small box of papers at a garage sale for $20. When contacted by the state, he resisted. He said this was the only piece that interested him in the whole box. He wanted his $20 back.

Questions to consider:

Is this a public document? Is there any evidence that an archives ever held it? What's the historical value? How can the State Archivist prove that it was stolen? How can the holder prove the right to hold it? What negotiating latitude do the applicable laws give the State Archivist? What negotiable solutions can you think of; what can the State Archivist do; what can the holder do? How would this case be different if it occurred in either of the other two states?

16. Notorious Letters

Ardent Collector received a phone call from the Curator of the James G. Blaine Presidential Library. Like all presidential libraries, it got its funding from a private foundation, but NARA administered it. Between 1864 and 1876, James G. Blaine, then one of Maine's Representatives in the House of Representatives, had written a series of letters to Boston businessman Warren Fisher Jr. implying that he, Blaine, had used his power as Speaker of the House to promote the fortunes of a small regional railroad. James Mulligan, Fisher's employee, testified before a congressional committee investigating the impropriety that he, Mulligan, had the letters and that they proved Blaine's corruption. Blaine got possession of Mulligan's letters and read them on the floor of the House in a successful defense of his behavior. Blaine ran for President in 1883, and his opponents published the "Mulligan Letters" expecting them to destroy Blaine in the eyes of the public. But Blaine won and became President in 1884. Ardent had two of the "Mulligan Letters" in his possession. The Presidential Library's Curator claimed they belonged with the others in the Blaine Library. He told Ardent to return them or he would sue.

Questions to consider:

Are these public documents? Is there any evidence that an archives ever held them? What's the historical value? Can the holder prove the right to hold it? What negotiable solutions can you think of; what can the State Archivist do; what can the holder do?

17. Prominent Brothers' Letters

15. Ardent Collector (Midline) had once had a serious fascination with the life and times of the first generation of state legislators of Midline, but the fascination had passed. He had systematically sold off various items over the past year to

allow him to collect in a new area. He had come to one of his favorites—and one of the first items in his collection—an 1812 letter from Paul LaVertu, then in the House of Representatives, to his brother, John LaVertu, first Governor of Midline. Paul wrote to tell John that he had successfully sponsored a bill to have a commemorative plaque placed at the site of John's bravery during a crucial battle and explaining his critical role in the Revolutionary War.

Ardent remembered buying the letter from Indifferent Dealer, and had not enjoyed the transaction. Indy put out a very attractive catalog, but his ultra-smooth ways had put Ardent off, and, in retrospect, the $3,000 Ardent had paid for the document seemed too much. Today, 15 years later, he thought $3,500 seemed a fair price. Ardent remembered Indy's saying that he had bought and sold the letter several times over the previous 20 years, and if Ardent ever wanted to sell it, he would happily handle it for him. Since then Ardent had become proficient at using an online auction service, and he posted it there. One of Meri Archivist's (Midline) Friends spotted it. Ardent was stunned and outraged when Meri contacted him. Collectors and dealers have bought and sold these items, through auction and catalogue, for decades with nothing but silence on the part of the state. Why, after all these years, did Meri think she could just show up and demand he hand over his own personal property? In his mind, the state had slept on its rights, and he would contact a lawyer to defend his right to sell them if he had to. That would cost him a lot of money, but he wouldn't just give them back. He was sorry he hadn't gone back to Indy, and told Meri as much.

Questions to consider:

Is this a public document? Is there any evidence that an archives ever held it? What's the historical value? Can the State Archivist prove that it was stolen? Can the holder prove the right to hold it? What negotiating latitude do the state laws give the State Archivist? What negotiable solutions can you think of; what can the State Archivist do; what can the holder do? How would this case be different if the State Archivist and the holder did not live in the same state? How would this case be different if they both lived in one of the other states?

Observations on the Cases

Below I have offered my thoughts on the cases, but you should not regard them as the definitive answers. Others may see other ways to address the problems.

I. Recognizing a Public Document

1. As incoming mail to the President, it is a public document.

2. As licences issued to a member of the public, these are not public documents.

3. As incoming mail to the Secretary of War, it is a public document, although the President did not write it as a public official, but as a father.

4. As outgoing mail, it is not a public document. Further, the President did not write it as a public official, but as a father.

5. As outgoing mail, it is not a public document.

6. As outgoing mail, it is not a public document.

7. As incoming mail to a quasi-governmental body, it could be considered a public document. However, given the traditions around and regular treatment of public documents at the time, a collector could argue that unless the government that would claim it (probably Massachusetts) can prove it was stolen, it should not be allowed to claim it based on modern archival theory.

8. As personal notes from which to speak, this is not a public document. The written resignation is the public document.

II. The Cases

1. Despite the lack of official stamps, letters between governors' offices are public documents. Trusty should call the state archives and alert them to these letters, including the thought that they might be forgeries. He should also notify the seller of the public nature of the letters and Softline's laws about public documents in private hands. He should not agree to buy or sell them until he knows a lot more about them.

2. Trusty should notify the seller of the public nature of the wills and the common but illegal nature of his great-grandfather's actions. Since these wills have never been on the market, he could also alert the Archivist of Virginia of the documents' existence. He should not agree to buy or sell them.

3. Short of sneaking the book across the state line and then selling it privately, Sally has no option but to return it to the archives. The fact that the archives hold Volumes 1 and 3 identifies Volume 2 as belonging there. Further, circumstantial evidence suggests that her late husband may have helped it leave the Penitentiary. No doubt the archives will stage a nice homecoming for the volume, as well as give Sally a receipt she can use for a charitable tax donation, but no more.

4. Sophie has very few options at this point. She could ask the dealers to negotiate for copies of the missing pages, which would restore the information in the volume. But with no leads on who has the pages or where, she has little hope of getting back the originals.

5. If the family wants to rid the house of its contents, Meri could offer to take the entire set of records from them. Otherwise she has no options. She's on a fishing trip with this visit; she doesn't know whether anything she will find evidence of additional thefts in those records. She has nothing she can demand under the law. If the family will not donate the papers, the laws of Midline will allow her to buy them.

6. Unless she's prepared to sneak the book across the state line and sell it privately, Agnes has no case. The archives has all the other books, and she does not know how her father got the book. The family has taken good care of it, and the laws of Midline allow Meri to repay Agnes for the conservation work her father had done to the book. No doubt they will stage a nice homecoming, but probably nothing more. Agnes cannot afford a lawyer to argue for some remuneration under the doctrine of accession which is discussed in chapter 6.

7. Hilda has a hard situation. The laws of her state give her no leeway to strike a deal with the bookseller. Because the bookseller lives out of state, Hilda would have to hire a lawyer in Softline to initiate a replevin action against the bookseller. That's very expensive, and given Softline's laws, she could not guarantee she would win. At best, Hilda's Friends would raise the roughly $1,000, buy the books, and then donate them to the archives.

8. Much as she would like to have these letters, Meri doesn't like the feeling that she's being put into a bidding war with other repositories; she has a very limited budget. Meri decides that the National Park Service should replevin the documents and deal with the Laudable decedents. She'll accept copies.

9. Meri should get a replevin action started as soon as possible. The book clearly belongs in the archives, and Indy now knows she wants it.

10. Meri's first impulse was to initiate a replevin action quickly, but something in Ardent's demeanor bothered her. She had to admit that he just happened to be the wrong holder at the wrong time. She did not want to stir up unnecessary hard feelings among the dealer and collector community, so she decided to accept copies, to complete the historical record, and let go of the originals. She gave him a letter relinquishing all claims to the originals.

11. Hilda has three choices. She can initiate a replevin action against Ardent, with no guarantee of winning. She can ask her Friends to buy them from Ardent and donate them to the archives. She can let them go. Her state laws do not allow her to accept copies.

12. Hilda will probably not get the support of the AG. The first action would involve forcing the auctioneer to reveal the buyer. The second would involve forcing the buyer to reveal to whom he sold them. The third would mean hiring legal help in the states in which the current holders live. She understands that this will get expensive, and she doesn't even *really* know what the bundles contained.

13. Trusty declines the offer. He knows that modern day Clerks of Courts never discard vital records. If they did truly discard them in the past, the modern clerk will still probably want this one back because of its display value. Trusty advises the decedents to offer it to Hilda and ask for a receipt that will entitle them to a tax deduction. They might also ask for some public recognition.

14. Sophie quickly realizes that the papers from the Governor's Commission papers qualify as public documents, but most of them probably don't qualify as archival. The few that might do not justify the illwill she could generate demanding them back. She decides to ask for copies of those that do, and a copy of the finding aid to the collection, so her researchers can benefit from the collection.

15. Sophia regarded $20 as a bargain. She couldn't throw a homecoming party for that amount.

16. Ardent refused. While historically significant, these are not government records and the Curator has no claim to them. The Blaine Library can get at the content of the letters through the 1883 publications that carried the story and the letters.

17. Meri backed off. She couldn't afford to pay his price, but she understood Ardent's legal position and recognized that she might not win. She agreed to accept copies, grateful that she could.

Note

1. Lincoln's son, then 12 years old.

Chapter 8

Avoiding Conflict

Avoiding a problem always costs less than remedying it. In this chapter, I describe precautionary measures for archivists, buyers, and sellers of historical materials who would prefer to avoid replevin. But first, two modern stories that could bring tears to your eyes.

1. In late May 2011, someone sent a notice to the Archives and Archivists listserv about a state that could not find 23 of 85 volumes of early land records. A reader on the list responded on May 25:

> Several years ago, I asked for permission to do some genealogical research in bound volumes of late 19th and early 20th century [deleted] court records. The county clerk at the time, who didn't know me from Adam, just handed me the keys to the county's warehouse where they stored their old records and excess courthouse furniture. Her only real concern was that I be sure to lock the door when I finished. Honestly, had it been my inclination, I could have backed a truck up and hauled off everything, or anything that I wanted.
>
> Because everything was so disorganized and there were no inventories, it was like looking for the proverbial needle in a haystack. I never did find the records that I needed. But much of what I did find was nothing less than astonishing, including a photograph of my grandparents, who for many years had managed the county's poor farm.
>
> Bound volumes of county records were stacked in piles on the floor, with some stacked almost to the ceiling. And the volumes were about the same size as the now lost state land records. So I can see how easily it could be that these lost volumes of state land records could easily have gotten mixed in unnoticed with other volumes of county records. [1]

2. I taught LIS7504, an online course on preservation management for Louisiana State University, during the summer of 2011. One of the students posted the following to a class discussion during the week of June 6–12:

> Having performed research in a number of archival repositories and governmental offices of public record in [deleted] throughout my adult life, I have become acutely aware of the danger in which countless items of cultural and legal significance are housed. Some of the Clerks of Courts' offices...for example, apparently have very lax if any, policies regarding the safety and integrity of legal documents, some of which date from the 18th century. I was shocked a couple years ago to "discover" amidst a pile of tattered documents of all ages in a former jail corridor a priceless artifact in the form of an 1868 voters' register, evidence of the first record of universal male suffrage—for all ethnicities—in [that] state! Knowing the genealogy and residency of most of the names entered therein, I could determine that as many as three-fourths of the men were recently emancipated, formerly enslaved persons. Just imagine the implications of this and similar documents and their importance in national history.

These stories contain huge errors in caring for historical records. Situations like these have caused many desirable documents to appear on the market. Were they stolen? Yes. Could the repository responsible for them have prevented the theft? Yes. With practices like those described above, the real miracle lies in how much material remains in those repositories.

We can easily pass judgment on the people and institutions represented above, but in fairness, we should consider the whole picture. No doubt those repositories lack staff with the knowledge and attitudes needed to care for historical documents properly. They also, obviously, lack the facilities and probably have no time in their schedules. All those inadequacies point back to their supervisors and the way they allocate their resources. We know how to avoid the vulnerability the records in the accounts above faced; the people in charge need the resources to provide a safe environment, and the people who supervise them must want the records to receive good care. Public documents belong to the public; ultimately, the public supervises their care through their willingness to pay for the resources to do that well. Care of public documents depends on how well the public will allow archivists to do their job. In other words, how well archivists can do their job comes down to how much the public will pay.

The Basics of Managing Historical Materials

Everything below that applies to researchers applies to staff as well. The vast majority of the thieves in historical repositories—I've heard statistics as high as 75–80 percent—work there.

First, historical repositories should document their holdings. The Council of State Archivists' (CoSA) own statistics indicate that across all the archives, only 37 percent have their holdings described at this basic level, "41% at a midlevel that includes some information about creator and content, and about 19% at a detailed level."[2] One can only assume that the repositories for smaller municipalities generally do even less well than state and federal repositories. In a perfect world, all repositories would identify and describe everything at a level that would make it easy for the archivist to find any particular record a researcher (or archivist) might want to look at. As an additional benefit, the holder of what might be a public document could go to the archivist's website and find evidence, if not conclusive proof, that the document should or should not be in the archives.

We live in a far less than perfect world, so problems occur around materials that a repository knows it has. 1) A repository may hold materials but no record of their chain of custody and the immediate source of acquisition. Without that record, the repository cannot show a clear title to the materials. 2) A repository may hold materials with confused provenance because of badly worded documentation about the acquisition of the materials. Badly worded or conflicting documentation also make a clear title difficult or impossible to show. Good inventory control in the form of complete records on the acquisition, processing, and management of the records can eliminate most problems. Good inventory control starts with having, and scrupulously following, a set of procedures that identify new materials coming into the archives. Therefore, establishing a minimum level of inventory control over the backlog seems like a fundamental task all repositories should chip away at. Today's archivist will not finish the work, but that's no reason to desist from it. Others will pick it up in their turn.

All historical repositories should take security very seriously. Good security starts with doors and locks and alarms, but it involves much more than that. A good security program closely monitors who has access to archival materials and how they handle them. It also guarantees that all materials return to their appointed place in the repository when the researcher has finished using them. It further guarantees that staff members do not have unmonitored access to materials at any time. With a good security system in place, an experienced thief might get away with stealing something, but not without a great deal of effort.

Thieves of historical documents steal for two reasons: 1) they want to own the materials, and so will take them home and keep them for themselves; 2) they want to sell them for the money. Materials stolen for profit may appear on the market fairly quickly; the others will probably not. Only after the thief can no longer care for them might they surface again.

All historical repositories have suffered losses. Upon discovery of the loss, embarrassment typically fuels a desire to hide the theft. Unfortunately, without good inventory control, a repository cannot know for sure what a thief might have taken. Repositories have found that wide publicity of known missing items has prompted the return of other—unknown—losses.[3] With that in mind, repositories should advertise their known losses to make it easy for collectors, dealers, and family members to recognize and return stolen materials they come across. Further, repositories should post large threatening signs about prosecuting thieves to the fullest extent of the law—and follow through with the threat. If, after the capture of a thief, the criminal justice system grinds unbearably slow, a civil action that the repository brings against the thief can provide the repository with the publicity it desires about its attitude on theft.

Avoiding Replevin

To avoid a replevin action, collectors and dealers should understand public records and public records law, and learn to spot public documents immediately. CoSA makes it easy with a web page that links to all the states that have their laws online.[4] When considering buying or selling a document, all parties involved could determine whether it came out of government custody by researching its provenance. Without background information provided by a thorough investigation of provenance before it acquired the materials and/or thorough documentation of the acquisition of its holdings, a collector, whether individual or institutional, may have trouble defending itself against convincing but conflicting claims of ownership. In the marketplace, the buyer should ask the seller to provide as much basic information about the provenance of the document as possible. Of course, in this less-than-perfect world, the holder may not have such detailed information. Ask these questions anyway.

1. How did the seller obtain the document? If the seller indicates that the document was passed down through his or her family, gather basic information about the story. Was the seller's ancestor really a Civil War participant, etc.? Some people enjoy providing this type of background information, but some do not. Reticence or inconsistencies may raise a red flag regarding the origins of the document and how it came to be on the market but does not constitute an infallible test. If the seller indicates he or she bought the document, the buyer may be able to verify that with the previous seller. Try to obtain the names of all previous owners and dates of ownership, in writing, for your own records. Documenting provenance will help to establish good title for any document. Of course, a lack of information does not mean that the holder of a document obtained it illegally.

2. Does an examination of the document itself raise suspicions? Government documents may have distinctive characteristics that convey their origins.[5] They may also have physical alterations made to hide their origins as government records. Look for erasures or areas cut out or trimmed. Also look for signs that the document was cut out of a book. While not conclusive proof of theft, such characteristics should raise concerns.

3. Is the document addressed *to* a government official? While archivists do not generally regard outgoing government documents as public records, they generally do look on correspondence addressed to state and local officials as public records. You should immediately inquire how and when documents of this nature left government custody.

4. Was the document—or those like it—ever deaccessioned from a government's holdings? In other words, does the archives have all other similar documents within its holdings?

5. Does the document have a history of being publicly bought, sold, traded, or referenced in a written sale catalog, journal, or other public reference or discussion?

6. If the donor wants to give non-government documents to the archives, ask why. Otherwise, a repository may wind up with donated materials but no clear statement of the donor's intentions for the gift. Without a statement of intentions or with a poorly worded statement about the donor's intentions, the repository may have difficulty defending a gift if someone challenges it.

While one or more characteristics in this list of questions will apply to the vast majority of government documents that appear on the market, a rare few do not have any of them. So the list serves as a guide, but not a definitive statement. Increasingly, state and national archives have websites that list records that have been identified as missing. The websites also have information about identifying government records. The CoSA website provides a link to the websites of every state and territorial archives.[6] Using these sites, a buyer may determine if the specific document in question is listed as being stolen or misappropriated from government custody. Unfortunately, only a small fraction of archival/historical documents that have been illegally alienated from government custody will be listed on the websites.

Investigating provenance, as suggested above, may result in dead ends or misleading information. Consulting the archivist of the government in question will give you the simplest way to determine whether a government document was illegally removed from government custody and whether a government archives wants it back. Each state archives has a designated individual to receive inquiries and to investigate issues related to municipal and county level documents for their state, in addition to state government records. The State Archivist's office can put you in touch with the right person.[7] The National Archives and Records Administration also makes similar contact information for investigating federal documents available.[8] In many cases, this investigation into the potential government interest in a document will verify that the archives does not have any interest in it. The archives may have appropriately removed it from government custody before the days of routine shredding, or it may have no interest in recovering the document for some other reason.

When you contact the designated person, provide a description of the document in question along with whatever information about its provenance you might have. A digital copy of all or some of the document (perhaps a few pages) would generally suffice. The archives will respond with their assessment of whether the document meets their criteria as an archival item, and if so, in which repository it most appropriately belongs. States have different procedures and varying latitude for negotiations if it decides to pursue recovery of the document. If the archives does not want the document, the State Archivist will notify the owner, in writing, that he or she has a clear title.

Many heirs, collectors, and dealers resist approaching an archivist, lest the archivist demand the document's return, especially where a document has a high market value. To make an inquiry without fear of facing an act of replevin, gather the information about the document(s) and ascertain the appropriate archives to contact. Give this information to an attorney, who will contact the archives in question, keeping you anonymous. You and the archives can then communicate through the attorney.

Good information to gather before contacting an attorney includes basic information about a document: 1) its date; 2) seller's name; 3) seller's address; 4) seller's phone; 5) seller's email; 6) document description (note erasures or cut outs); 7) state and governmental subunit of document's origin; 8) federal, state, or local document. Beyond these basic descriptors, answers to the following questions can be useful: How did the seller come into possession of the document (provenance)? Do/did the seller or the seller's immediate family work for the government entities listed in items 7 and 8? If the seller purchased the document, who sold the item to him/her and what is that person's contact information? If you have contacted the archives or officials that may be responsible for the document's origin, summarize the response.

Contacting the appropriate state archives when selling a government document from that state will clarify important information about the document, e.g., whether it was stolen or appraised as archival. Talking with the archives will undoubtedly help to clarify the provenance of the document and establish good title to it.

To avoid the expense and negative publicity of a replevin action, archivists, where the laws allow it, can develop policies for accepting copies of alienated materials. Most alienated documents do not have such high historical or symbolic value that they warrant the cost of a replevin case, and a copy will fill the gap in the historical record.

Pursuing Replevin

Archivists considering filing a replevin action against a dealer or collector should ask the following questions: 1) Does irrefutable proof of our ownership exist? 2) In the absence of clear documentation of ownership, does a convincing body of circumstantial evidence exist? 3) Is the document worth going to court over or would a copy provide the information as well? 4) Is the publicity of any struggle over the materials going to help or hurt the reputation of your repository or its working relationships with dealers, collectors, and other repositories in the area? 5) Is there some way to settle this out of court?

Collectors, which include non-governmental archivists and curators, who receive notice that they hold a public document that the government archivist wants back have a number of issues to consider. 1) Is the claim irrefutable? 2) Is the document worth going to court over? 3) Is any publicity a struggle over the material going to help or hurt our reputation?

If an archivist decides to pursue a case through the courts, the fight should occur on home turf. State courts tend to respect the laws of their own states. Other states' laws may vary enough that an iron-clad case in the home state might fail in another. Further, going to court in your home state will cost less. Each state has an Attorney General's office to represent you; you'll need to hire a local attorney if you fight the case in another state.

Before you go to court, be sure your enabling legislation says what you believe it says, and that it covers the material you want covered. Be as sure as you can be that the legislative intent is clear. In other words, make sure the law does not have a hole that the opposing lawyer can make use of.[9]

Trudy and Gary Peterson's guide to legal matters for archivists provides good detailed procedural advice on how to work with a lawyer on replevin cases. While written from the perspective of and for an archivist, everyone will find something useful in it. SAA includes it in its collection of electronic publications.[10]

I repeat, avoiding a problem always costs less than remedying it. Avoiding the necessity for a replevin action takes conscientious documentation and management of their holdings by archivists, collectors, and dealers. Given the resources to establish and follow procedures outlined above, everyone should make that effort.

Notes

1. May 25, 2011, http://forums.archivists.org/read/?forum=archives (April 15, 2011).

2. Council of State Archivists, *The State of State Records: A Status Report on State Archives and Records Management Programs in the United States* (Iowa City, Iowa: Council of State Archivists, 2007), 34, http://www.statearchivists.org/reports/2007-ARMreport/index.htm (15 April 2011).

3. Mary Boone Bowling in the audio recording of Session 705, "Theft Transparency in the Digital Age: Stakeholder Perspectives," presented during the annual meeting of the Society of American Archivists, Chicago, August 27, 2011.

4. "The Sale of Certain Government Records Is Illegal! Please Check the Law," http://www.statearchivists.org/issues/publicrecordssales/laws.htm (Sept. 16, 2011).

5. "Identifying U.S. Government Documents," http://www.archives.gov/research/recover/identifying-government-documents.html (Nov. 15, 2009).

6. Council of State Archivists, Directory of State and Territorial Archives and Records Programs, http://www.statearchivists.org/states.htm (Sept. 16, 2011).

7. Directory of State and Territorial Archivists and Records Managers.

8. NARA, "Recover Lost and Stolen Documents: Contact the National Archives," http://www.archives.gov/research/recover/recover-documents-contact.html (Sept. 16, 2011).

9. David Cheever, "Whose Document Is It, Anyway? Replevin and the Marketplace," in the audio recording of Session 105 presented during the annual meeting of the Society of American Archivists, Austin, August 13, 2009.

10. Gary M. Peterson and Trudy Huskamp Peterson, *Archives and Manuscripts: Law* (Chicago: Society of American Archivists, 1985), 92–93, http://www2.archivists.org/sites/all/files/Archives&Mss-Law.pdf (June 15, 2011).

Bibliography

Adams, Randolph G. "The Character and Extent of Fugitive Archival Material." *American Archivist.* 2, no. 2 (April 1939): 85–96.

Alabama. Code of Alabama. Section 41-13-21. http://alisondb.legislature.state.al.us/acas/CodeOfAlabama/1975/41-13-21.htm.

American Philosophical Society. http://www.amphilsoc.org/about.

Barrow, William J. "Deacidification and Lamination of Deteriorated Documents, 1938–1963." *American Archivist.* 28, no. 2 (April 1965): 285–290.

Bauer, G. Philip. "Public Archives in the United States." In Hesseltine and McNeil, *In Support of Clio*, 49–76.

Baumann, Roland M. "Samuel Hazard: Editor and Archivist for the Keystone State." *Pennsylvania Magazine of History and Biography.* 107, no. 2 (April 1983): 195–215.

Behrnd-Klodt, Menzi L. *Navigating Legal Issues in Archives*. Chicago: Society of American Archivists, 2008.

Belk, Russell W. *Collecting in a Consumer Society*. New York: Routledge, 1995.

Benjamin, Mary A. *Autographs: A Key to Collecting*. New York: Bowker, 1946.

Benjamin, Walter. *The Collector.* 51 (February 1937).

Berkeley, Edmund, Jr. "The Language of Autograph Collecting." In Berkeley, Klingelhofer, and Rendell, eds., *Autographs and Manuscripts*, 53–62.

Berkeley, Edmund, Jr., Herbert E. Klingelhofer, and Kenneth Rendell, eds. *Autographs and Manuscripts: A Collector's Manual*. New York: Charles Scribner's Sons, 1978.

Bishoff, Liz, and Nancy Allen. *Business Planning for Cultural Heritage Institutions: A Framework and Resource Guide to Assist Cultural Heritage Institutions with Business Planning for Sustainability of Digital Asset Management Programs*, CLIR Report 124. Washington, DC: Council on Library and Information Resources, January, 2004. http://www.clir.org/pubs/reports/pub124/pub124.pdf (24 April 2011).

Boles, Frank. *Selecting and Appraising Archives and Manuscripts*. Chicago: Society of American Archivists, 2005.

Boles, Frank, and Julia Marks Young. "Exploring the Black Box: The Appraisal of University Administrative Records." *American Archivist*. 48, no. 2 (Spring 1985): 121–140.

Bowling, Mary Boone. In the audio recording of Session 705, "Theft Transparency in the Digital Age: Stakeholder Perspectives," presented during the annual meeting of the Society of American Archivists, Chicago, August 27, 2011.

Brichford, Maynard. *Archives and Manuscripts: Appraisal and Accessioning*. Chicago: Society of American Archivists, 1977.

"Brief History of the American Antiquarian Society." http://www.americanantiquarian .org/briefhistory.htm.

"Brief history of NAGARA." http://www.nagara.org/displaycommon.cfm?an=1.

Brown, Ellen Firsching. "What Happens When Uncle Sam Comes Calling for Your Collection?" *Fine Books and Collections* 8 (September/October 2008): 31-35.

Burke, Frank G. "The Future Course of Archival Theory in the United States." *American Archivist*. 44, no. 1 (Winter 1981): 40–46.

Burnette, O. Lawrence, Jr. *Beneath the Footnote*. Madison: State Historical Society of Wisconsin, 1969.

Burckel, Nicholas C. "The Society: From Birth to Maturity," *American Archivist* 61 (Spring 1998): 12–33.

California Government Code. Title I Division 7 Chapter 3.01 Section 6204 (a) (2). http://www.leginfo.ca.gov/pub/09-10/bill/asm/ab_1201-1250/ab_1245_bill_20091011_chaptered.html.

———. Section 1. Chapter 3.01 (commencing with Section 6204) is added to Division 7 of Title 1 of the Government Code of California. Official California Legislative Information. http://www.leginfo.ca.gov/pub/09-10/bill/asm/ab_1201-1250/ab_1245_bill_20091011_chaptered.html.

Cappon, Lester J. "Historical Manuscripts as Archives: Some Definitions and Their Application." *American Archivist*. 19, no. 2 (April 1956): 101–110.

Cheever, David. "Whose Document Is It, Anyway? Replevin and the Marketplace." In the audio recording of Session 105 presented during the annual meeting of the Society of American Archivists, Austin, August 13, 2009.

Cole, John Y. *Ainsworth Rand Spofford: Bookman and Librarian*. Littleton, Colo.: Libraries Unlimited, 1975.

———. *For Congress and the Nation: A Chronological History of the Library of Congress.* Washington, D.C.: Library of Congress, 1979.

———. *Jefferson's Legacy: A Brief History of the Library of Congress.* Washington, D.C.: Library of Congress, 1993.

Connors, Thomas. "Appraising Public Television Programs: Toward an Interpretive and Comparative Evaluation Model." *American Archivist.* 63, no. 2 (Spring/Summer 2000): 152–174.

Cook, J. Frank. "The Blessings of Providence on an Association of Archivists." *American Archivist* 46 (Fall 1983): 374–399.

———. "'Private Papers' of Public Officials." *American Archivist.* 38, no. 3 (July 1975): 299–324.

Cook, Terry. "Mind Over Matter: Towards a New Theory of Archival Appraisal," in Craig, *Archival Imagination*, 38–70.

Council of State Archivists. Directory of State and Territorial Archives and Records Programs. http://www.statearchivists.org/states.htm.

———. Directory of State and Territorial Archivists and Records Managers. http://www.statearchivists.org/statearchivists.htm.

———. *Profiles of State Archives and Records Management Programs.* Iowa City, Iowa: Council of State Archivists, 2007.

———. *Report of the Blue Ribbon Panel: A Supplement to* The State of State Records: *A Status report on State Archives and Records Management Programs in the United States*. Iowa City, Iowa: Council of State Archivists, 2007. http://www.statearchivists.org/reports/2007-ARMreport/BRPreport-final.pdf.

———. *The State of State Records: A Status Report on State Archives and Records Management Programs in the United States*. Iowa City, Iowa: Council of State Archivists, 2007.

Cox, Richard J. "American Archival Literature: Expanding Horizons and Continuing Needs, 1901–1987," *American Archivist* 50 (Summer 1987): 306–323.

Craig, Barbara L., ed. *The Archival Imagination: Essays in Honour of Hugh A. Taylor.* Ottawa: Association of Canadian Archivists, 1992.

Danielson, Elena S. *The Ethical Archivist.* Chicago: Society of American Archivists, 2010.

"D.A.R. Desires Virginia to Take Action to Recover Martha Washington's Will." *New York Times.* Jan. 7, 1914, 2.

Dunlap, Leslie W. *American Historical Societies, 1790–1860.* Madison, Wisc.: Privately Printed, 1944.

England. Museums, Libraries, and Archives Council. *UK Export Licensing for Cultural Goods: Procedures for Exporters of Works of Art and Other Cultural Goods, a Museums, Libraries, and Archives Council Notice*. London: Museums, Libraries, and Archives Council, 2010. http://www.mla.gov.uk/what/cultural/export.

Ericson, Timothy. "At the Rim of Creative Dissatisfaction: Archivists and Acquisition Development." *Archivaria.* 33, no. 1 (1991–92): 66–77.

Fleckner, John. "'Dear Mary Jane': Some Reflections on Being an Archivist." *American Archivist.* 54, no. 1 (Winter 1991): 8–13.

Forbes, Malcolm. *More Than I Have Dreamed: A Lifetime of Collecting*. New York: Simon & Schuster, 1989.

Gamerman, Ellen. "The Case of the Disappearing Documents." *Wall Street Journal*. Sept. 30, 2011, http://online.wsj.com/article/SB10001424052970204422404576596873383476078.html?mod=ITP_fridayjournal_0.

Georgia State and Court Records (O.C.G.A. 50-18-102) and Local Government Records (O.C.G.A. 50-18-99). http://sos.georgia.gov/archives/how_may_we_help_you/policy_statement/default.htm.

Gilliland-Swetland, Luke J. "The Provenance of a Profession: The Permanence of the Public Archives and Historical Manuscripts Traditions in American Archival History." *American Archivist.* 54, no. 2 (Spring 1991): 160–175.

Griffin, Burt. "Lewis and Clark II: A Legal Analysis." *Manuscripts.* 10 (Winter 1958): 64–67, 72–73.

Grondahl, Paul. "Records from Governors are Slow in Coming." *TimesUnion.Com*. June 12, 2011. http://www.timesunion.com/local/article/Records-from-governors-are-slow-in-coming-1420344.php.

Gutherie, Kevin M. *New York Historical Society: Lessons from One Nonprofit's Long Struggle for Survival*. San Francisco: Jossey-Bass, 1996.

Hackman, Larry J., and Joan Warnow-Blewett. "The Documentation Strategy Process: A Model and a Case Study." *American Archivist*. 50, no. 1 (Winter 1987): 12–47.

Ham, Gerald. "Report of the Secretary, 1969–70." *American Archivist* Volume 34, Number 1 (January 1971): 92–100.

Harris, Michael H. *History of Libraries of the Western World.* Metuchen, N.J.: Scarecrow Press, 1995.

Hesseltine, William B., and Donald R. McNeil, eds. *In Support of Clio: Essays in Memory of Herbert A. Keller.* Madison: State Historical Society of Wisconsin, 1958.

"Historical Writings: The Independent Value of Possession." *The Yale Law Journal*. 67, no. 1 (Nov. 1957): 151–163.

"History of CoSA." http://www.statearchivists.org/about.htm#history.

Holmes, Oliver W. "Public Records—Who Knows What They Are?" *American Archivist.* 23, no. 1 (January 1960): 3–26.

International Council on Archives. Committee on Electronic Records. *Guidelines for Managing Electronic Records from an Archival Perspective.* ICA Study 8 (February 1997): 1–58. http://www.ica.org/en/node/30019.

Johnson, Edward. *The Wonder-Working Providence of Sion's Savior in New England 1628–1651.* 1653.

Jones, H. G. *Historical Consciousness in the Early Republic.* Chapel Hill, N.C.: North Caroliniana Society, 1995.

———. *The Records of a Nation: Their Management, Preservation, and Use.* New York: Atheneum, 1969.

Kane, Lucile M. " Manuscript Collecting." In Hesseltine and McNeil, *In Support of Clio*, 29–48.

Kolsrud, Ole. "The Evolution of Basic Appraisal Principles—Some Comparative Observations." *American Archivist.* 55, no. 1 (Winter 1992): 26–39.

Land, Robert H. "Defense of Archives Against Human Foes." *American Archivist.* 19, no. 2 (April 1956): 121–138.

Library of Congress. *Report of the Librarian of Congress, 1897.* Washington, D.C.: Government Printing Office, 1897.

Library of Virginia. "The Sale of Government Records Is Illegal!" http://www.lva.virginia.gov/public/replevin.htm.

Lowenthal, David. *The Heritage Crusade and the Spoils of History.* Cambridge: Cambridge University Press, 1998.

———. *The Past is a Foreign Country.* Cambridge: Cambridge University Press, 1985.

Lutz, Paul V. "Government Loses Suit for Documents." *Manuscripts.* 19 (Fall 1967): 9–11.

Maass, Richard. "Arguments Heard in the Clark Case." *Manuscripts.* 8 (Winter 1956): 113–116.

Maher, William J. "Issues and Prospects for the National Archives," *Perspectives* (September 1999) http://www.historians.org/perspectives/issues/1999/9909/9909not2.cfm.

Maine. "Involved in the Purchase or Sale of Government Records? It's Illegal! Please Consider the Following" http://www.maine.gov/sos/arc/replvnot.htm.

Maine. Revised Statutes Title 5: Administrative Procedures and Services: Part 1: State Departments: Chapter 6: State Archivist Heading: Pl 1973, C. 625, §16 (New) §92-A. Definitions. http://www.mainelegislature.org/legis/statutes/5/title5sec92-A.html.

McCoy, Donald R. *The National Archives*. Chapel Hill, N.C.: University of North Carolina Press, 1978.

———. "The Struggle to Establish a National Archives in the United States." In Walch, *Guardian of Heritage*, 1–15.

McKemmish, Sue, and Michael Piggot, eds. *The Records Continuum: Ian Macleans and the Australian Archives First Fifty Years*. Clayton, Australia: Ancora Press, 1994.

Metzdorf, Robert F. "Lewis and Clark I: A Librarian's Point of View." *Manuscripts*. 9 (Fall 1957): 226–230.

Metzger, Oliver. "Making the Doctrine of *res extra commercium* Visible in United States Law." *Texas Law Review*. 74 (1996): 615–653.

Michigan Department of History, Archives, and Libraries. "eBay and Archival Collections." http://www.michigan.gov/hal/0,1607,7-160-15479-127674--,00.html.

Miller, Fredric M. "The SAA as Sisyphus: Education since the 1960s." *American Archivist*. 63, no. 2 (Fall/Winter 2000): 224–236.

Mock, Sanford J. *Document Stories: A Pastiche of Stories*. Los Angeles: Elton-Wolf, 2002.

Muensterberger, Werner. *Collecting: An Unruly Passion*. Princeton: Princeton University Press, 1994.

Museums, Libraries, and Archives Council, *UK Export Licensing for Cultural Goods: Procedures for Exporters of Works of Art and Other Cultural Goods, a Museums, Libraries, and Archives Council Notice*, (London: Museums, Libraries, and Archives Council, 2010), www.mla.gov.uk/what/cultural/export/~/media/Files/pdf/2010/AELU/UK_Export_Licensing_guidance_for_exporters_of_works_of_art_and_other_cultural_goods.ashx (May 13, 2011).

National Archives and Records Administration. "Help the National Archives Recover Lost and Stolen Documents." http://www.archives.gov/research/recover/#q3.

———. "Recover Lost and Stolen Documents: Contact the National Archives." http://www.archives.gov/research/recover/recover-documents-contact.html.

———. "Recover Lost and Stolen Documents: Identifying U.S. Government Documents." http://www.archives.gov/research/recover/identifying-government-documents.html.

New Jersey Department of State. Public Records and Archives. "New Jersey Missing or Alienated Records of the State of New Jersey Public Notice." http://www.nj.gov/state/darm/links/missingdocuments.html.

New Jersey. New Jersey Statutes 47:3–16. http://www.njarchives.org/links/pdf/pl1953c410.pdf.

New Mexico. 14-5-1 to 14-5-10 NMSA 1978. "Public Records Recovery Act." http://www.nmcpr.state.nm.us/info/14-5NMSA.pdf.

Newsome, Albert Ray. "Uniform State Archival Legislation." *American Archivist.* 2, no. 1 (January 1939): 1–17.

Norton, Margaret Cross. "Some Legal Aspects of Archives." *American Archivist.* 8, no. 1 (January 1945): 1–11.

O'Neill, James E., "Replevin: A Public Archivist's Perspective." *College and Research Libraries.* 40, no. 1 (January 1979): 26–30.

O'Toole, James. "On the Idea of Permanence." *American Archivist.* 51, no. 1 (Winter 1989): 11–25.

———. "The Symbolic Significance of Archives." *American Archivist* 56 (1993): 234–55.

O'Toole, James M. and Richard J. Cox. *Understanding Archives and Manuscripts.* Chicago: Society of American Archivists, 2006.

Panitch, Judith M. "Liberty, Equality, Posterity? Some Archival Lessons from the Case of the French Revolution." *American Archivist.* 59, no. 1 (Winter 1996): 30–47.

Pearce, Susan M. *On Collecting: An Investigation into Collecting in the European Tradition.* London: Routledge, 1995.

Peterson, Gary M., and Trudy Huskamp Peterson. *Archives and Manuscripts: Law.* Chicago: Society of American Archivists, 1985. http://www2.archivists.org/sites/all/files/Archives&Mss-Law.pdf.

Petersen, Scott. "Another Perspective on Replevin." *Rail Splitter.* 10, no. 1 and 2 (Summer/Fall 2004): 4–6.

Peterson, Trudy H., Patrick M. Quinn, and Hugh A. Taylor. "Professional Archival Training." *American Archivist* 40 (July, 1977): 315–20.

Pierce-Moses, Richard. *A Glossary of Archival and Records Terminology.* Chicago: Society of American Archivists, 1985. http://www.archivists.org/glossary.

Pinkett, Harold T. "Investigations of Federal Recordkeeping, 1887–1906." *American Archivist.* 21, no. 2 (April 1958): 178–192.

Posner, Ernst. *American State Archives.* Chicago: University of Chicago Press, 1964.

———. "Archival Administration in the United States." In Posner and Munden, eds. *Archives and the Public Interest*, 114–130.

———. and Kenneth W. Munden, eds. *Archives and the Public Interest.* Washington, D.C.: Public Affairs Press, 1967.

Presidential Records Act (PRA) of 1978. http://www.archives.gov/presidential-libraries/laws/1978-act.html.

Price, William S. "N.C. v. B.C. West, Jr." *American Archivist.* 41, no. 1 (January 1978): 21–24.

Public Archives Commission of the American Historical Association. *Annual Report of the American Historical Association for the Year 1900: Vol. II: Report of the Public Archives.* Washington, D.C.: Government Printing Office, 1901.

Purcell, Aaron D., "Abstractions of Justice: The Library of Congress's Great Manuscripts Robbery, 1896–1897." *American Archivist.* 62, no. 2 (Fall 1999): 325–345.

Rapport, Leonard. "No Grandfather Clause: Reappraising Accessioned Records." *American Archivist.* 44, no. 2 (Spring 1981): 143–150.

Rendell, Kenneth. *History Comes to Life: Collecting Historical Letters and Documents*. Norman, Okla.: University of Oklahoma Press, 1995.

Rhoads, James B. "Alienation and Thievery: Archival Problems." *American Archivist*. 29, no. 2 (April 1966): 197–208.

Rosenbach, Abraham S. Wolf. *Books and Bidders*. Boston: Little, Brown, 1927.

Samuels, Helen Willa. *Varsity Letters*. Metuchen, N.J., and London: Society of American Archivists and Scarecrow Press, 1992.

Shelley, Fred. "Manuscripts in the Library of Congress: 1800–1900." *American Archivist.* 11, no. 1 (January 1948): 3–19.

Smiley, David L. "The W.P.A. Historical Records Survey." In Hesseltine and McNeil, *In Support of Clio*, 3–28.

Smith, John. *The Generall Historie of Virginia, New-England, and the Summer Isles*. 1624.

Smithmeyer, John L. *History of the Construction of the Library of Congress, Washington, D.C.* Washington, D.C.: Beresford, 1906.

Society of American Archivists, "A*CENSUS," American Archivist 69 (Fall/Winter 2006): 406. http://www.archivists.org/a-census/ACENSUS-Final.pdf (1 May 2011).

———. Annual Meeting, August 13, 2009, Washington, D.C. Sessions 105 and 205.

———. "So You Want to Be an Archivist: An Overview of the Archives Profession." http://www2.archivists.org/profession.

"State of North Carolina vs. B.C. West." *Manuscripts.* 28, no. 2 (Spring 1976): 114–124.

Sung, Carolyn Hoover. *Peter Force: Washington Printer and Creator of the American Archives.* Ph.D. diss. George Washington University, 1985.

Talley, Marcia. "Morris Leon Radoff: The Man and the Monument." *American Archivist* 44 (Fall, 1981): 331.

Taylor, John M. *History in Your Hand.* Westport, Conn.: Praeger, 1997.

Tennessee. State Library and Archives. "Replevin." http://tennessee.gov/tsla/aps/replevin.htm.

Texas State Library and Archives Commission. "Sale of Government Records." http://www.tsl.state.tx.us/arc/sale.html.

Turrini, Joseph M. "The Historical Profession and Archival Education," *Perspectives* (May 2007), http://www.historians.org/perspectives/issues/2007/0705/0705vie2.cfm (1 April 2011).

United States War Department. *The War of the Rebellion: A Compilation of the Official Records of the Union and Confederate Armies.* Series III, Vol. IV. Pasadina, Calif.: Historical Times, 1985.

Upward, Frank. "In Search of the Records Continuum in Ian Maclean's 'Australian experience' Essays in Recordkeeping." In McKemmish and Piggot, *Records Continuum*, 110–130.

Van Tassel, David D. *Recording America's Past: An Interpretation of the Development of Historical Studies in America, 1607–1884.* Chicago: University of Chicago Press, 1960.

Walch, Timothy, ed. *Guardian of Heritage: Essays on the History of the National Archives.* Washington, D.C.: National Archives and Records Administration, 1985.

Walt Whitman Archive. http://www.whitmanarchive.org.

"Want J.P. Morgan Sued for Relic." *New York Times*, Jan. 7, 1914.

"Will Sue J.P.Morgan for the Stolen Will of Martha Washington." *Columbus* [GA] *Daily Enquirer*, Jan. 8, 1914.

Winthrop, John. *The Journal of John Winthrop.* 1630.

"Would Indict J.P. Morgan." *New York Times*, Jan. 8, 1914.

Young, Julia Marks. "Annotated Bibliography on Appraisal." *American Archivist.* 48, no. 2 (Spring, 1985): 190–216.

Index

About the Author

Elizabeth Dow grew up helping with the work on her family's dairy farm in central Pennsylvania. After graduating with a B.A. in history and teaching credentials from Juniata College in Huntingdon, Pa., she taught English and American History to 7th graders in northern Maryland. She earned a Master of Library Science degree from the University of Oregon in 1970. She then developed an elementary school library which she ran for twelve years in Morrisville, Vt. She bought her first computer, an Osborne I, in 1982.

During her years in Morrisville, Dow completed the course work on an M.A. in history at the University of Vermont. Before she finished her thesis, she received a fellowship for a Ph.D. in Library Science from the School of Library and Information Science at the University of Pittsburgh. While at Pitt, she worked in various positions at the Western Psychiatric Institute and Clinic. She took more courses from the Information Science department than the Library Science Department, and for her last class she took a course in archival theory taught by David Bearman. That course focused her clearly on archives as her career path. In five years at Pitt, Dow completed both her M.A. and her Ph.D., then she immediately returned to Vermont to take a job at the Sheldon Museum in Middlebury, Vt., creating MARC records for a large collection of 19th century materials.

From the Sheldon she moved to the Vermont State Archives on a grant-funded position to process the papers of a former governor. While there, she introduced MARC cataloging. When the grant ended, she accepted a position in Dana Medical Library at the University of Vermont. From there she moved to University of Vermont's Special Collections Department where she started encoding finding aids in EAD in 1998. She also managed a project to develop the George Perkins Marsh Online Research Center, linking EAD and TEI encoded documents.

In 2001, Dow moved to Louisiana State University to develop an archives program in the School of Library and Information Science. While at Louisiana

State University she received two large grants from the Institute for Museum and Library Services, to improve archival education at both the graduate education and continuing education levels in Louisiana and along the Gulf Coast. She has written two books prior to this one, *Creating EAD Compatible Finding Guides on Paper*, and *Electronic Records in the Manuscript Repository*, both published by Scarecrow Press. In 2011 LSU promoted her to the rank of Professor.

CPSIA information can be obtained at www.ICGtesting.com
Printed in the USA
BVOW041214300412

288979BV00002B/1/P

9 780810 883772